I'm just getting started and so far I have laughed, wiped away a tear, and been inspired!

—**Donna Chumley**, Tate Publishing

Spunk, love, fun, and stubborn! These are just a few words that come to mind when I think of Beth. She definitely leaves a stamp on your heart and makes my job worthwhile. Thanks, Beth, for letting me in. Much love and many blessings.

—**Rita Gutierrez**, R.N.

The greatest thing about Beth is her passion for life. She has been through much adversity, yet she manages to be a caring and concerned friend. Beth will always ensure those she cares about know they are loved by her. God blessed my life with knowing Beth; she has made me strive to be a better nurse.

—**Sondra Patton**, R.N.

Faith, determined, loving, friend are words that describe someone special. Having Beth in your life is always a new adventure. Many days her smile is what lifts my spirits and gives me a reason to go on. Wondering what she might do next is always an adventure that I love to share with her. She has blessed my life, and I feel fortunate to be someone involved in Beth's life. May God bless you, Beth, and know I love you!

'inda **Kepley**, R.N.

D1521311

Beth is the most pure and kind-spirited person I have ever known. Her book shows how one deals with adversity. Her courage and positive, uplifting Christian attitude despite multiple obstacles make her heroic in my eyes. She may not be able to physically touch her surroundings, but the whole world now will truly be touched by her story."

—**Geoffrey Burton Plumlee**, M.D.

For me, Beth's friendship has been a blessing from God. The story of the life she has led is amazing! You will surely be moved as you read her story. Watching how her strong faith has brought her through is truly humbling.

—**Jennifer Talbert**, CMA

RISING
ABOVE

Karen —

Thanks for sharing your
knowledge of painting with
us. I've enjoyed your classes
so much! Hope you enjoy
reading Beth's story —

Janet Damon

RISING ABOVE

Facing the Dragon of Neurofibromatosis

Janet Damon

With Contributions by Beth Brandt

TATE PUBLISHING
AND ENTERPRISES, LLC

Published by Tate Publishing & Enterprises, LLC
127 E. Trade Center Terrace | Mustang, Oklahoma 73064 USA
1.888.361.9473 | www.tatepublishing.com

Tate Publishing is committed to excellence in the publishing industry. The company reflects the philosophy established by the founders, based on Psalm 68:11,
"The Lord gave the word and great was the company of those who published it."

Book design copyright © 2012 by Tate Publishing, LLC. All rights reserved.
Cover design by Shawn Collins
Interior design by April Marciszewski

Published in the United States of America

ISBN: 978-1-61862-712-4
Biography & Autobiography / Personal Memoirs
11.12.29

DEDICATION

For John, who saw Beth with the eyes of love, and that love has made all the difference.

ACKNOWLEDGMENTS

Thanks to God, who brought us through the fire time after time. Thank you for inspiring Beth that her story should be told and for allowing me the privilege of writing it. A big thanks to Tate Publishing for believing in the project; you are wonderful folks with whom to work.

I am especially grateful for my husband, Darrel, my family, and my friends. Your love and support helped make this book a reality. And a special thanks to my sister, Shirley, for all your help and encouragement.

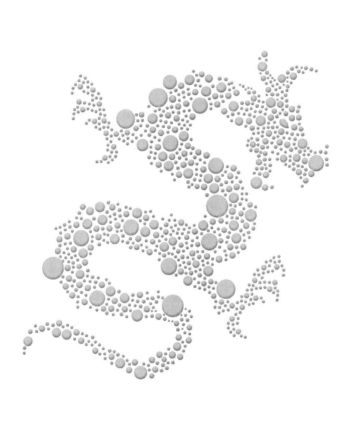

TABLE OF CONTENTS

FOREWORD

Many biographies express the challenge an individual endures to become great in the eyes of the world, while others express the power of Christianity in an individual's life, which allows then an ever-persistent faith, calmness, and peace in good times and in the face of pending defeat.

In *Rising Above*, Janet Damon captures both, demonstrating the innate human desire to live a fulfilled life on earth while adhering to Christian biblical principles. This is the only formula for true success. This book details a young woman's desire to do both, and how a roadblock (neurofibromatosis) significantly altered the former while simultaneously strengthening the latter.

I had the privilege of meeting Beth Brandt on August 23, 2007, when her mother (the author of this book) brought her to my office. What a blessing! I have studied her medical history fairly extensively over the last three years but was unaware of the longevity and severity of her physical challenges (causing mental challenges for her as well) that started at a very young age.

I have always been amazed at Beth's ability to maintain a sweet and loving attitude in spite of her situation. This was multiplied exponentially while reading *Rising Above*. It also increases with each of our weekly visits, where her giving and tender spirit is consistently demonstrated. She might bring the whole staff candy or have a joke and smile, ready to brighten our day.

Beth has an unspoken, peaceful presence that touches those blessed with the privilege to know her. Her endless string of challenges has resulted in relentless tenacity to triumph over adversity, displaying unwavering strength rather than a questioning of her Christian faith. Her continued positive attitude is an inspiration to me and countless others, proving that God has an eternal purpose with Beth's life, drawing all of us closer to Him.

This book is a "must read" for all neurofibromatosis victims and their families; anyone with physical or mental challenges; or for those needing a boost of strength in their Christian faith, hope, and love.

May God bless you, Beth. Thanks for being a part of our lives.

—**Forrest W. Saxon**, Doctor of Chiropractic

PREFACE

My thoughts jostled together like corn in a popper as we bumped speedily along the rough highway. I was in the passenger seat of the ambulance as it rushed toward the hospital, carrying my precious daughter, Beth, in a desperate attempt to reach the hospital in time to save her life following a horrendous automobile crash about an hour earlier.

Would we make it in time? Would she live? How serious were her injuries? I tried to pray, but my heart seemed to have been squeezed into a hard piece of ice. I was so afraid for Beth.

As she was driving home from work that evening, an unlicensed, illegal immigrant, out on parole for another offense, driving a borrowed car with no insurance, and speeding at 70 mph, had T-boned Beth's car right on the driver's side door. Her car was airborne over 200 feet from the highway and landed in a freshly plowed, muddy field. Thank God for the softer landing.

In a senseless panic, the driver ran and yanked open the passenger-side door and dragged Beth's unconscious body over the center console and onto the ground. Then he pulled her through the muddy field and draped her body over an irrigation pipe. He said later he was afraid the car would burst into flames. For this, we have to give him credit for some degree of mercy.

Suddenly, I heard the nurse's voice call out from the back. "Can we pull over? We can't get any vitals on the patient."

My heart almost stopped. "Oh, God! Help!" Then the Scripture came to mind from Romans 8:26 (NIV): "We do not know what we ought to pray for, but the Spirit Himself intercedes for us with groans that words can't express." What a comfort that was! If I ever needed help, it was at that moment.

Soon we were rumbling up the road again toward St. Catherine's Hospital in Garden City, Kansas, some seventy miles away. I became aware again of the rough ride we were having, and I wondered how sick and injured patients survived it.

My thoughts returned to the plans my husband, Darrel, and I had for a business trip to California. We were packed and ready to leave the next morning. It seemed so unimportant now. Beth was all that mattered. Would she survive this and be able to walk and work, to fulfill her dreams of love and marriage? She already had more physical problems than most people have to deal with in a lifetime, and now this!

Many thoughts rushed through my mind: Beth as a baby, then a toddler, laughing and playing; hearing the diagnosis of neurofibromatosis with all the accompanying fears and emotions; watching her leave for school each day; kissing her ouchies and comforting her when she fell; and I wondered, *What next?* Our amazing girl was so resilient; she just didn't give up. Would this accident destroy her grit? Or would she bounce back the way she always had before?

OUR BABY, BETH, ARRIVES

On August 28, 1962, a new baby girl entered the world. Beth Anne Brandt, 6 lbs 14 oz, joined our family, becoming the second daughter of Gunther and Janet Brandt of Boise City, Oklahoma. Beth looked yellow, so she was placed under a special light to correct the jaundice. Her grandpa Dixon remarked that her little nose appeared to be made of wax.

Holding her and examining every inch of her little body, as all mothers do, I discovered several brownish spots and splotches on her skin; but when I asked Dr. Wheeler, he assured me they were only birthmarks, nothing to be concerned about. We had no idea these signaled the presence of neurofibromatosis, a condition that would ultimately change the course of her life. At least we had about four years in which to enjoy her without knowing anything about what lay ahead.

As a baby, Beth was fussy, crying a lot. She also suffered from constipation or diarrhea almost constantly. Her skin was so sensitive that even the gentlest touch when cleaning her would cause her to bleed. She didn't sleep a night through until she was nine-and-a-half-months old, and even then, it was a rare treat for us when she did.

When she learned to talk, she often complained of itching. Otherwise she was a happy, friendly little tyke, smiling and waving at everyone.

At birth, her hair was dark, but it was soon replaced by little blonde, curly ringlets. She began walking at the age of ten months, and she seemed to be growing and developing normally. As she got older, she began to fall a lot. She was pigeon-toed, so she would trip over her own feet and fall, throwing her head back so she wouldn't hit her face, causing cuts or bruises under her chin all the time.

Beth never met a stranger. She was an adorable, cute, friendly little girl who was never afraid of strangers or dogs. She would toddle right up to them to pet or hug them, assuming they loved her as much as she did them. She only got bitten twice, and neither was serious.

Beth wrote about her life a few years ago, and I'd like you to hear her story in her own words:

> I was born on August 28, 1962. I was normal except I had jaundice. Mom said I was a fussy baby, cried a lot, and was a blessing when I was asleep. I was born with café au lait spots; my parents were told they were harmless birthmarks. At age 4, I was diagnosed with Von Recklinghausen Syndrome,

also called Neurofibromatosis. When I was four years old, I had deformities of both feet and legs, so I was fitted with leg braces that I wore until age eight. The braces were attached to my shoes, keeping me from losing them. That was not the purpose for them; they were to correct the turning in of my feet.

I don't really recall those years except having to wear bulky, ugly shoes.

SIBLINGS, CHILDHOOD FUN, AND CHALLENGES

At the time of her birth, Beth had one older sister, Diane, then two years old. Diane loved her new baby sister and was always a willing helper, running to get diapers, washcloths, or whatever was needed. She also loved holding Beth, with supervision, of course.

When Beth was four years old, another sister joined the family. Kerri Jan was born on February 1, 1966. Then, when Kerri was eleven months old, my older sister, Kathy Junell, was killed in a car accident in Amarillo, Texas. Kathy and I were close, and she had stated in her will that in case of her death, she wanted us to take her children and raise them. Her first husband had died, and she was single at the time of her death.

There were three children in Kathy's family: Denise, who was seven years old; Jim, who was six; and Greg, who was three. Now we had Denise, 7; Diane, 6; Jim, 6; Beth, 4; Greg, 3; and Kerri, 11 months. You can well imagine this was quite an adjustment for the entire family. Denise and Diane were both used to being the eldest child; neither wanted to give up that place. Diane was just six months older than Jim. And our family had doubled overnight!

Suddenly, Beth had to adjust to having five siblings instead of two, and sharing everything more, especially her parents' attention. The additional three children had just lost their mother, so naturally they needed extra love and reassurance as well. Beth needed special time and attention, as the NF was beginning to cause changes in her body. Her knock-knees and pigeon toes caused falls often, and her coordination was never good, making it difficult for her to do anything requiring fine-motor skills.

This frustrated her a lot as she struggled to accomplish various tasks such as cutting, coloring, and learning to print. She didn't understand these changes, and I didn't either very well, but I did what I could to comfort and reassure her of my love, her worth, and her secure place in the expanded family.

The older kids became more supportive and protective of Beth once they had adjusted to having their lives turned upside down. The main friction as children was between Beth and her younger sister, Kerri, but that was normal sibling rivalry.

With patience and lots of love, we made it through the transitions. The kids got along remarkably well on the whole, and they soon came to think of each other as brothers and sisters, rather than cousins. We could see the change of heart between the kids, especially in the following incident involving Beth.

We lived about four blocks from the grade school, and the kids always walked to and from school. One day Beth came running in the house all happy and excited, because when some kids had been picking on her on the way home, Jim told them if they picked on her again, he would beat the tar out of them! She and I were both happy and surprised by Jim's protectiveness. When I told Jim I was so proud of him, he grinned from ear to ear!

Beth and Kerri used to play Barbie dolls a lot. They had a Barbie swimming pool, and one day Beth was barefoot, stepped on glass, and cut her foot. She remembers that she ran and stuck her foot in the water in the Barbie pool! I can imagine that Kerri wasn't too pleased about that!

As a child, Beth enjoyed playing Red Rover with her siblings, hide-and-seek, which she played with the dog, and other outdoor games, as well as swimming. As she got older, she liked to read and work jigsaw and word-seek puzzles.

Beth has a lifelong love of children and animals. From the time she was a toddler of three or so, any time we would be in a crowd, she would go and find any babies or children younger than herself and come back with the name and age of each one. She always said what she wanted to be when she grew up was a mommy and a veterinarian, but life had a different path for Beth.

Buying shoes for Beth was always a challenge. As a baby, she would curl her toes when I tried to put her shoes on her, making it difficult. As she got older, her feet grew so fast, becoming quite large, as is common with NF, and she was really hard to fit with shoes, but I did the best

I could. Her feet were so wide it was nearly impossible to find a pair of shoes that fit properly. Taking her shoes off one evening, I discovered her little feet were actually bleeding! I cried, thinking how much they must have hurt and that she just kept playing! When I asked our doctor why she wouldn't have said anything to me about it, his answer was that she lived in pain all the time, so she was used to it. You can just imagine how that made me feel!

Beth always adored her daddy. She would run and wrap her arms around his legs the minute he walked in the door, wanting him to pick her up. But he, being of the old, stoic German ancestry and never showing much emotion, would unwind her, push her away, and ask, "What's for dinner?"

When she was four years old, she went out into the back of the greenhouse, which was attached to our house, and she proceeded to break stacks of terra cotta pots. I was busy in the house and had no idea she was doing this. Gunther caught her in the act and gave her a hard spanking. Beth came running to me, tears streaming down her little face but smiling ear to ear!

"My daddy spanked me!" she declared happily.

I later told Gunther he should be ashamed that his little girl wanted his attention so bad that she was thrilled to have even the negative attention of a spanking. It took many years before Gunther seemed to understand her struggles in the face of NF. The learning disabilities, the poor physical coordination, and the gradual appearance of more tumors weren't noticed by him as they were by Beth and me. She so longed for his attention, and it was heartbreaking to watch her try so hard to win it.

With the combined family of six growing children, often chaos and squabbling broke out in our house. When

Beth and Kerri got mad at each other, they would run into another room and slam and lock the door in the other's face. They loved teasing Jim and aggravating him. They used to take his favorite toy, Smokey Bear, away from him and hide it. Or, knowing he was scared of the dark, they would lock him in the basement and turn off the lights, the switch being on the outside. You can see by these anecdotes that Beth was a normal, happy, somewhat mischievous child.

A huge part of Beth's life is her love of animals. She always loved spending time on my parents' farm, as there were lots of animals there. She especially loved to ride the horses, and my dad always had at least one gentle one for the kids to ride. When I drove up to get the girls after their having been at the grandparents' for a couple of days, four-year-old Beth saw me coming and stood in the middle of the gate, shaking a little fist and stamping her foot, yelling, "Darn! Darn! Darn!"

When I remarked that she didn't seem very happy to see me, she said she hadn't gotten to ride the horses as much as she wanted, so she wasn't ready to go home.

DARK SHADOWS

At four years old, a mysterious bump appeared on the inside of Beth's left wrist. It was very soft, about the size of a dime, and about half an inch high. I took her to our family doctor, and he assured me it was only a little fatty tumor, nothing to worry about. But he could see I was concerned, so he made us an appointment with a dermatologist in Amarillo, Texas. (We later understood that we needed to take her to a neurologist, but neither our doctor nor we knew that at the time.) I took Beth to this appointment, and after examining the bump and other signs, he called his colleague in to help solve the problem. Then they brought out their books, studied them carefully, and discussed the diagnosis. Finally they returned to us with, "She has Von Recklinghausen's syndrome."

"What is that?"

"Neurofibromatosis." They could just as well have been speaking in Chinese!

They tried to explain the condition and what to expect. They told us that NF is always inherited, that it could go back several generations, that there is no treatment and no cure. They had no idea how it could progress or what problems it might cause her in the future. I asked every question I could think of, trying to understand what we were dealing with. I was not reassured, to say the least, and left for home with a knot in the pit of my stomach.

This began many years of studying and seeking information on neurofibromatosis. One of the first facts uncovered was that it is not always hereditary, as we had been told, and that half the cases are caused by the spontaneous mutation of a gene during the baby's development before birth. The half that is hereditary can only come if there is a first-degree relative having the condition. Of course, I asked what a first-degree relative meant and was told, "Father, mother, sister, brother." That settled the origin of Beth's NF; it was spontaneous. One answer was found; many more questions remained.

Now I began to learn some of the complications brought about by NF. (This abbreviation is easier for us than writing out the name each time. But do not confuse neurofibromatosis with necrotizing fasciitis, which is abbreviated the same way.) Some of the many complications NF can cause are: dwarfism, growing extra tall, bone deformities, extra-large heads, tumors on the optic nerves, tumors on the auditory nerves, susceptibility to various types of cancers, scoliosis, knock knees, pigeon toes, epilepsy, learning difficulties in children of normal or above normal intelligence, chronic pain, and many more.

Also included is skin sensitivity, which we had noticed from birth. The presence of five or more café au lait spots at birth is a sure sign the baby has NF. These are spots, splotches, or freckles that are the color of coffee with cream, thus the name.

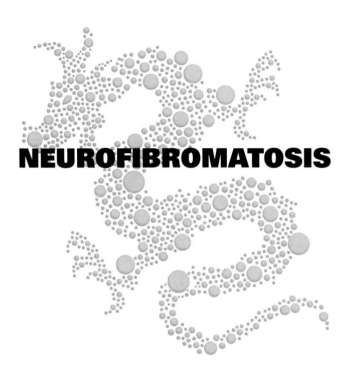

NEUROFIBROMATOSIS

I feel a simple explanation of NF would be helpful to the reader. This is my best definition of NF1 (there are also NF2 and schwannomatosis, but Beth has NF1). Neurofibromatosis is a progressive disorder of the central nervous system, which causes tumors to grow on the coverings of the nerves anywhere inside or on the surface of the body. Fifty percent of cases are hereditary, and fifty percent are spontaneous, meaning they are caused by the spontaneous mutation of a gene on chromosome 17 during the baby's development before birth. NF is always congenital; if you aren't born with NF, you will never have it. It is not contagious.

No two cases of NF are alike; they range from being so mild the person only has a few of the café au lait spots, to causing serious deformities of the bones and skin to life threatening things such as cancers, loss of one or both eyes, deafness, to serious debilities of many kinds.

There is no predictor of who may have NF, although there is now a pre-natal test that shows if the baby will have it. This was not available before Beth's birth, but even if it had been, I would never have considered abortion, which is what some recommended. And why would I even think of being tested, when we had never even heard of the existence of such a disorder?

There also is no predictor of how any given case of NF will progress. Some people live their whole lives with only a few brown spots or bumps, while others face life-threatening challenges all along the way. Some win their battles; others do not and die prematurely from NF related causes. One thing a lot of NF sufferers have in common is that they have multiple surgeries. Beth has had so many surgeries related to NF that we have lost count of them, beginning at about the age of thirteen and continuing until the present time.

The tumors appear in greater numbers at certain times of life, such a puberty, pregnancy and menopause. If a woman has NF, the chances are 50 percent that any child she bears will also have it; if both husband and wife have NF, the chances increase to 75 percent. But there has been so little information and education about Neurofibromatosis that even a lot of the people who have it do not know this.

NF is considered a disorder of the central nervous system; it is *not* a disease. There is no satisfactory treatment, although some are now being treated with chemotherapy. Beth has had numerous tumors removed, but most of them grew back. Unless the doctor knows a lot about the condition and is very careful to get all the roots, they grow back again, usually larger than before. There is no cure ... yet!

I'm glad there is more information available now. When we first heard Beth's diagnosis, there was very little information available at all.

Normally, the body produces a specific protein called Neufibromin, a tumor suppressor. NF sufferers' bodies do not produce this vital protein, thus the tumors grow. Perhaps someday, research will find a way to help NF patients produce Neufibromin

If you desire to learn more about NF, and we hope you will, you can find specific contact information in the afterword.

The more I learned about NF, the more overwhelming the diagnosis seemed. One of the first things we did for Beth was to take her to a doctor who checked her feet and legs and ordered torsion braces for her. These consisted of tension rods or coils that extended from her waist to her feet, on the outside of her legs.

There was a belt that buckled around her waist, then there were straps that buckled below her knees, and the metal was bolted to the bottoms of her shoes. She began wearing these at four years old and wore them for four years, of course having to get new ones as she grew. She rather liked them because she was bad about losing one shoe, and with these, her shoes were tied together, so one never got lost! The function of them was to keep tension on her feet to correct the in-turned or pigeon-toed walk. They did help a lot.

Beth started school wearing these braces, and she wore them through third grade. She felt self-conscious about wearing them but doesn't remember any of the kids making fun of her about them. I have noticed that the younger children are, the more they accept differences among them. She said she hated wearing heavy, ugly shoes, but they did help prevent a lot of falls.

The braces Beth wore were fitted by a doctor in Wichita. I remember one trip there to get larger shoes for her. We were in the shoe store, and a lady of around sixty years came in who had neurofibromatosis. Her entire face was a mass of tumors, and I felt almost panicky, thinking, *Oh, please, God, don't let that be Beth's future!* Although her face wouldn't ever have that many tumors, she would have much more serious problems.

EARLY SCHOOL YEARS

Beth started kindergarten on her fifth birthday, August 28, 1967, and she received a stuffed lion for that occasion. She loved that thing and insisted on carrying it with her to school every day! Finally, her teacher asked her to leave it at home.

In first grade, Beth came home one day just beaming, telling me, "Mama, I think Mrs. English [her teacher] likes me! She called me 'honey' today!"

My answer was I sure wished she had called her that on the first day of school, since it brightened her day so much!

When she started to school, Beth had a real struggle trying to learn math. We learned that she had dyslexia, as do many children with NF. Her case was different from the norm in that reading and spelling came easily to her, but when she did math, the numbers appeared to jump around, and she just couldn't do the problems.

Her second-grade teacher told me that she thought if Beth's dad would help her with math, she would do much better. I told him, and he did help her—one time. That one time, she managed to work every problem correctly! Sadly, he never took the time to help her again.

Let's let Beth tell you a little about her early school years:

> Since I was diagnosed with dyslexia, I had trouble with math. My first-grade teacher always asked me if I left my thinking cap at home in the sugar bowl. My second-grade teacher gave me a swat every day that year, probably because I was always talking. Teachers didn't need parental consent then, so my mom was not told by them and certainly not by me! I told her after I was grown, and when she asked why I didn't tell her at the time, I told her because one swat was enough. I sure did not want more when I got home!
>
> My third-grade teacher, Mrs. Strong, tutored me in her home a few times a week. She did not allow the use of erasers at her house, and if I tried to use one, she could see through walls and I'd get caught.

In third grade, the teachers talked it over and decided Beth should be put into the special education class. They called me in to tell me, and I said, "Absolutely not! She doesn't need that. She is as capable of learning as any other child. She just needs a little extra help with math because of the dyslexia!"

They argued; I stood firm. At that time, in Boise City, Oklahoma, the special education teacher was a sweet, very heavy woman, Mrs. T. She would take the kids in her class to her house and teach them to sweep and mop floors, dust, wash dishes, fold clothes, etc. Sometimes she took them to the grocery store, got food, and taught them to cook simple things. (One of the older girls in her class told me she felt that the teacher really just used the kids to do her work for her.) I told the teachers I taught my girls all those things at home; I was sending them to school to be educated in reading, writing, math, history, geography, etc.

When the dust settled, Beth stayed in her class, and she went to her teacher Virginia Strong's home after school a few times a week for tutoring in math.

Every teacher she ever had knew me; I was up at the school a lot! I was never rude or loud, but I stood up for my kids!

> Since I had been diagnosed with dyslexia, in fifth grade they put me in a special reading class. One day the teacher, Miss Moon, handed me a cassette tape player. I was to listen to the tape and follow their instructions. I had not seen a tape player before and was not told how to use it, so I turned it over to see if there were instructions on the bottom of it. I got caught, was told that was cheating, and Miss Moon grabbed me by the ear and yanked me from my seat. She then had the male math teacher give me a swat, as she didn't have the nerve to do it herself.

When I came back in the room, the other kids were concerned for me. They were asking me if I was all right, and I smiled and said I was, because I didn't want to give Miss Moon the satisfaction of knowing I was really hurt. Not from the swat, but my ear hurt really badly.

When my mom found out this was done to me, she went to the school and shook her finger in the teacher's face and told her, "Don't you *ever* touch my child again!" She said if I needed punishment, God provided a place for a swat, and it certainly wasn't my ears! A few years later it was found I had hearing damage to that ear because of this incident.

School days were normal except they sent me once a week to a room where they did physical testing. These tests consisted of crawling through a tunnel, passing a large ball back and forth between hands, and walking on a balance beam. They hoped the exercises would help my coordination, and maybe they did help a little bit.

Of course, none of my teachers had ever heard of NF and didn't know anything about the problems it causes. We were just learning about them as we went along too. I really hope that by now, teachers do understand more about it and are more understanding and compassionate. We do not ask for any special treatment, but kindness and compassion go a long way toward making a child feel comfortable, and that makes it much easier to learn.

I went to Girl Scout camp and, along with my friend Tammy Overbay, did my share of pranks, like pulling a sleeping camper from her tent, then putting her hand in warm water so she would wet her bed; fooling around, hoping to get out of digging the hole for the latrine—but that job was saved just for us, anyway.

When I was eight, I went to Bible camp for a week. I enjoyed it, so I never got homesick. My cousin, Barbara Miller, went too, and we were close when we were kids. We both went to Good News Camp several summers and would wind up sharing a room. We would each take a bottom bunk and buy shoestring cherry-flavored licorice, and tie it on the top bunk springs so we could have a snack in bed. We took out a canoe and took an unexpected bath when it capsized! Once when we were riding horses, mine got spooked, and I fell off into poison ivy. I didn't have too many of the bumps (tumors) at this age, so I wasn't yet self-conscious about wearing a swimsuit in front of other kids.

The year I was eight, I accepted Jesus as my Savior at Good News Camp. This was the best decision of my life! Ever since that day, I have known that God loves me and has protected me.

More Family Changes

Gaining three additional children, the worries about Beth's increasing health problems, needing but postponing several surgeries to correct both of her knees and both of her feet, the continual increase of neurofibromas on her body, her learning problems and poor coordination all combined to increase the stress in our household. Gunther was mostly an absentee father and usually emotionally absent even when physically present.

There were so many things we needed to talk out and work through, but he just wouldn't talk to me about them. He just could not seem to give me the emotional support I so desperately needed, and I didn't feel I should have to make all the decisions about Beth's health care by myself. Eventually this drove a wedge between us, and we were divorced after fourteen years of marriage.

Jim elected to stay with Gunther, and the girls went with me. We moved to Ulysses, Kansas, where we had relatives. After being in Ulysses for several years, I met and eventually married a great, supportive, loving man named Darrel Damon.

Junior High School Years
—Beth—

We moved to Ulysses, Kansas, just in time for me to start seventh grade. I did not like having to start to a new school in a new town, having to go to school with people I did not know, and having to make new friends. These kids hadn't grown up with me and didn't know the tumors came on gradually. When you have NF, it causes tumors to grow on the coverings of the nerves, any-where, inside or outside the body. These tumors can range in size from pinhead size to huge. By this time I had tumors on my arms and hands, and hundreds of them on my back. They usually don't cause pain but are sometimes sensitive and cause a lot of itching, which can be embarrassing.

These tumors grow wherever there is a café au lait spot (a spot the color of coffee with cream), with a great increase in their number at certain phases of life, such as puberty, pregnancy, and menopause. Once they appear, they never go away on their own but can be removed surgically and even then often grow back larger than before.

So while the kids in Boise City accepted me and didn't treat me as "different," the kids in Ulysses looked at me and saw only the bumps. I didn't make friends easily, and was different physically, on the outside where it could be seen, so that made it even harder to make new friends.

By this time I had several tumors that could not be covered up. This earned me the names "Lumpy" and "Camel" and "Tumor," and a few I'd rather not repeat. I did make a few friends; some I still talk to today.

The number of tumors kept increasing, and I walked with an awkward gait because of the knock-knees and pigeon toes, so it wasn't hard for the kids who liked to pick on me to find something to make fun of me about. I tried to ignore the taunts and just get along with everyone as best I could.

One incident I recall was when I decided to mark through the dirty words on the bathroom stalls at school. I was doing this with another girl, and we got caught and were made to scrub the walls in the bathroom plus the limestone wall on the end exit. I was not punished at home because Mom believed I was being honest when I told her I was marking the words out, not adding to them. I didn't realize until we got caught that she was writing more dirty words as fast as I could scribble them out!

Mom became friends with our neighbors behind us. They attended the First Assembly of God Church and invited us kids to special Children's Crusade services they were having. We enjoyed it a lot, and after that we all started attending this church. In Boise City, we had attended the First Baptist Church. Kerri and I were baptized and became members of the Assembly along with the rest of the family. I was thirteen when I was baptized. My faith helped keep me calm when kids teased and made fun of me. I knew I had a friend, Jesus, who sticks closer than a brother, and He helped me every time I called on Him.

I remember going to the front of the church one Sunday and asking the pastor to pray for my feet because they were hurting so much. He was very kind, took off my shoes and socks, and really prayed for my feet to be healed. I have believed for my healing ever since I accepted the Lord, and I still expect God to heal me!

Eighth grade wasn't any better than seventh; one thing that happened in P.E. that I remember is the trampoline incident. We were to use a safety belt and do a flip. Everyone in the class was to stand around the trampoline and be spotters and catchers. The kids dared me to do a flip without the belt; I did, and my class all moved back and let me fall on my head. Not a soul was concerned about me, and not one person asked me, "Are you okay?" I heard lots of laughter. If not for the awkwardness caused by the NF, I probably could have done the flip without incident.

I had become acquainted with a girl named Shirley, who was in my class, and she and I had become friends, but she was absent that day. I really believed she was my friend, but what she did to me proved it only worked her way. She had punched some plastic circles out, put them in a little bottle of water, and then told me they were contact lenses. She wanted me to put them in my eyes and see if it helped my vision. I am very nearsighted. I fell for her lie; I was dumb enough to believe her, and I put them into my eyes, and one got stuck and scratched my cornea. I should have known something was wrong when she didn't put them in her own eyes.

My eye hurt really badly, and after school my mom took me to the local eye doctor; he couldn't get it out, so she had to take me the next day to an ophthalmologist in Dodge City. The plastic thing had migrated to the top of my eyeball, and he managed to remove it. I had to wear an eye patch for several days while my cornea healed; surprisingly, I did not get teased about it. Shirley's mom punished her by making her bring over $10 of her own money to help pay for the gas.

Another thing Shirley and I used to do was to get into trouble intentionally, so we would be sent to detention. We liked staying after school together. Mom wondered why I remained friends with Shirley when she got me into trouble often and wasn't always nice to me, but I have always been able to forgive easily, and even a not-so-good friend is still a friend, and because of the NF problems that made me different, I felt I didn't have any friends to spare.

On a school field trip out to Wagon Bed Springs, some kids were chasing me and throwing eggs at me. I climbed up into a tree to try to get away from them. I don't remember any of the eggs actually hitting me; I guess they weren't very good shots.

One thing I hated about P.E. class was having to undress and shower in front of the other girls. I was very embarrassed because of the NF nodules on my body, so the P.E. teacher, Miss Judy Mills, kindly allowed me to use a private shower stall with a curtain. God bless her!

One time, the other girls stole my bra and hid it. I couldn't find it, and I felt self-conscious, so I wore my jacket the rest of the day. By this time, I was getting a lot of tumors on my breasts, which added to my discomfort and embarrassment.

Before I was promoted from the eighth grade, I was checked over by the Kansas Crippled Children's Foundation, and it was determined that my knock-knees could be corrected surgically. I finished eighth grade, and soon after school was out, I went to Wichita and had surgery on both knees. They went in, removed a small bone, and put it back in crosswise to make my legs grow straight. They could not have done this if I had stopped growing, as further growth was necessary for the legs to straighten.

When I came back to my room after surgery, I had a smile and a joke for Mom, which surprised her. I had a roommate, a younger girl who had had part of her leg bones removed because she was growing too fast! I didn't understand that, but I did understand her pain and confusion, and Mom and I prayed for her.

While in the hospital, when the doctor came on his rounds, he was accompanied by a whole group of student doctors and interns. None of them had ever seen anyone with NF, so they were being educated about this condition. They all stood around my bed talking and asking the head doctor questions, as if I were invisible and deaf, or incapable of answering questions myself. I really didn't like how this made me feel. They came in once a day, every day, while I was there. They made me feel like a bug on a pin!

MORE ADJUSTMENTS

It was hard at first for Beth to make friends in Ulysses, because she felt self-conscious. But gradually, some came to see the sweet person she was, and she had a few good friends. Janice Allmon was one of the first, and Maurine Sullivan and Debbie Alexander followed. One boy who was always kind to her was Brian Neatherlin, whom she had known in Boise City. His family moved to Ulysses around the same time as ours. Another girl who was always kind and took up for her when others picked on her was Olga, who now owns The Goody Shop in Ulysses. Several of the girls were always kind, but very few of the boys.

Beth has always made friends easily with anyone who looked beyond the skin to see the wonderful girl within.

She maintains her friendships over many years but is now only able to stay in contact by phone, with help. Still, there are a faithful few who make the effort to stay in contact with her.

I remember so well taking Beth to buy shoes for her eighth-grade promotional exercises. This is (or was!) usually the time in a young girl's life when she got her first pair of grown-up, high-heeled shoes, and I was so hoping to be able to find at least one dressy pair of shoes for her to wear with her new dress.

When we walked into the shoe store, the owner said, "Oh, no! Not that kid with the huge feet again!" Well, if it had not been the only shoe store in town, we would have walked right back out the door! We looked at every pair of women's shoes, but nothing fit her wide feet. Then, with a sinking heart, I took her over to the men's section, where we finally purchased a pair of plain white men's sneakers. I cried all the way home while Beth valiantly tried to comfort me.

A few years ago, at the Home Products dinner in Ulysses, a former schoolmate came over and asked Beth's forgiveness for all the mean things she'd done to her back in school. This was Jolene Zirkle Heckman; and the strange thing was, Beth couldn't remember Jolene ever being mean to her! Another classmate sent her a nice card several years after graduation, also asking forgiveness. Beth doesn't seem to have held grudges against anyone who mistreated her.

—Beth—

My first job after my seventh-grade year was roguing in the sorghum fields. We had to walk between the rows and use a knife to cut off the "bastard" heads, those that were taller than the others. These fields were for genetic seed, and those heads would contaminate the seed. I hated that job; it was hot, itchy, and because of my coordination problems it was hard for me to keep up. Plus, I was assigned to a crew of girls from school who hassled me unmercifully.

I got a job working in the daycare center, where I was assigned jobs like scraping paint off the windows and pulling weeds. When I asked why I couldn't work with the kids, I was told they (supervisors) were afraid the kids might "catch" NF from me. This is a prime example of adult ignorance. Why didn't they just *ask* me? I have loved little kids all my life; I would never put one in danger. I was finally allowed to walk them to the pool, but only one time.

It was after this that I worked at Western Prairie Care Home. And while I was in college in Liberal, I worked at the care home there.

PETS

Beth loved animals as much as she loved little kids, and we always had pets around. Cats and dogs, of course, also rabbits, and we had one dog that would round up the rabbits when Beth and Kerri took them out of their hutches to eat the clover that grew wild around there. He never hurt any of the rabbits; he was just their protector.

When she was about fourteen, Beth got a spider monkey, which she named Toby. That monkey was a constant source of amusement and frustration. Spider monkeys have no thumbs, but that doesn't diminish their ability to use their hands! Toby learned to unfasten her cage and would run around the house until we caught her and put her back. We had to devise more difficult locks for the cage. What that monkey couldn't get into, a grown person with tools probably couldn't either. Once I was making pies for a church bake sale. I had my crusts all baked and set on the counter to cool. I had to go to town for something, and when I came back, my crusts were crumbs, scattered all over the place. The upper cabinet doors were standing open and sugar, food coloring, coffee, tea, flour and spices were opened and thrown down. Mixed amongst that mess were broken dishes. I had some plants hanging in the window in macramé hangers, and they had been dumped, the dirt mingling with the sugar, flour, etc. Toby was swinging on the macramé hanger as happy as could be!

Oh, I was aggravated and frustrated! I grabbed that monkey and threw her out into the raging snowstorm. A couple minutes later, I looked out the window and saw her huddled on the porch, tail wrapped around herself, shivering. I said, "Freeze, you little devil!" (Of course I didn't mean it.)

The school bus came just then, and Beth scooped Toby up, put her inside her coat, and came in, trying to hide Toby and giving me a *look*. Of course I forgave Toby— after the mess was cleaned up. But the church had to do without a couple of pies.

When I told a friend, Med Mead, about why I didn't have pies to bring, she asked, "Is that monkey still alive?"

Oh, how Beth loved that monkey! She considered her as important as the other members of the family! And Toby got attention for herself and her owner, making Beth feel more accepted by her peers.

Beth's love for all animals was the reason she chose being a veterinarian as her future career. Unfortunately, the steadily advancing NF and its accompanying problems didn't allow that to happen. She later wanted to become a trainer of horses and dogs as therapy animals, and she would have been good at it. She hoped to land a job working in a zoo and applied for one in Colorado Springs but wasn't hired. She said she would be willing to muck out the cages or whatever if she could just work with the animals.

We also had some other unusual pets: a white-tailed deer, an antelope, a "deodorized" baby skunk that the kids named Spunky, various caged pets such as hamsters, and Beth also had a black and white mouse that she named Mickey.

Beth always wanted a horse, so we purchased her an older gelding from Everett Stutzman. While Dunnie was gentle and safe for the kids to ride, he didn't like to be caught. It took all of us to corner him and get a bridle on him. Then he would get up close to any fence he saw and try to scrape the rider off. But Beth loved him, and we kept him for several years. By this time, Beth was in junior high school, and she tried her best to train that horse, thinking it would help with her future plans of becoming a vet/trainer. But he was old and stubborn, and she didn't make much headway with him.

HIGH SCHOOL YEARS

—Beth—

I started freshman year on crutches because of the recent surgery, in a school that was confusing to get around in, as it is built in a circle. It was not easy changing classes and having to carry around a lot of books, not knowing where the classes were, and not any offers of help. This was before backpacks. I remember being in line for school pictures and one male classmate, K.B., decided there was nothing wrong with me, so he kneed me in the back of my legs, knocked me down, and tossed my crutches out of my reach. After he did this, I heard maniacal laughter.

One of my female peers brought my crutches back to me and helped me to my feet. I really appreciated her kindness.

When I was a little kid, I had always thought it would be fun to be on crutches. It sure didn't take me long to learn that was not the case!

I was baptized in the Holy Spirit when I was about fourteen, and knowing I could call on the Lord for help anytime and anywhere made the taunts of my classmate seem less important. I knew that if anything should happen to me, I would go to live in heaven with Jesus. This confidence made me feel stronger and more able to cope with whatever life might bring my way.

Shirley and I continued to be friends. We had our share of fights, but for the most part we got along very well. Her mother was very controlling, though, and had Shirley write me a letter full of lies. I could tell she really didn't want to give it to me but was under her mother's control. This letter stated that I was a bad influence on Shirley, and she was not to be friends with me. The truth is that she was a bad influence on me, or would have been, but I would not be like her nor do the things she did. The big difference between us was that I knew Jesus and was being shown the right way to live; and she was wild and "sowing her oats," as the saying goes. I am so glad I had Jesus as my Savior; He was always with me in times of stress and trouble, giving me comfort and the courage I needed to keep going. I called on Him often, especially at school. I'm so glad I can pray and He can hear, even if I never utter one word aloud!

I remember that during my freshman year, there was a great increase in the number of tumors, or neurofibromas, as they are known medically. I was thankful that most of them were where my clothing covered them. They were getting too numerous to count, especially on my back. The tumors kept increasing continually on my arms, hands, legs, and feet too. They are various sizes, from pinhead size to the size of half a baseball.

The summer after my freshman year, I returned to Wichita for more surgery, this time on both feet. This surgery was to correct my pigeon-toed walk. At this time they also removed several of my larger tumors, one being the one on my left wrist. I sort of missed that one, as it was my quick way of telling which was my left hand! Another was on my left shin. Both have grown back, but the one on my wrist is not as large as it was before. I wanted to see what they looked like after being removed, and they said it was waste matter and could not be allowed. I was really upset.

My mom stepped in and told them, "She doesn't want to keep it; she just wants to see it."

Then they did bring it to me to see. It was all wrinkled up and funny looking, not at all like it had looked before removal.

My mom always tried to keep a happy face on for me, and she bet me that the first thing I would say when I came out from under the anesthetic would be, "Oh, my feet hurt!" But I said no, it wouldn't; and it wasn't! What I said was, "Hi, Mom, I'm back!"

This foot surgery required me to have casts on both feet, and I was not to put any weight on my feet at all. So we borrowed an old wooden wheelchair that reclined. After six weeks, I went in to have the casts removed, but to my disappointment, they had to redo them, and I had to wear them for another three weeks.

While I was wearing the casts, Mom would put a five-gallon bucket upside down in the bathtub, so I could sit on it with my feet outside the tub, and she could shower me with the hand-held shower wand.

My sister Denise got married that summer, and I had to attend the wedding in the wheelchair, wearing casts.

They had put two metal pins in each foot, inserted from the bottoms of my heels. These were about the size of sixteen penny nails. When they went to remove them, they said, "She doesn't need pain medicine, these will slip right out."

Wrong! The intern who removed them had to use pliers, brace both his feet against the table I was on, and had his back against the wall. They did not "slip out," as the bone had grown to them, and my screams proved it. Once they came out, they were followed by a stream of blood the size of the pins. The nurse was complaining that I was making a mess.

The doctor heard her and said, "You are the nurse, and she is the patient; it is your job to clean up the mess, so do it!"

When I was younger, one of my doctors had taught me about using my "pain button." He had me put the tip of my forefinger on the top of my bent thumb and press, telling me it would help my pain. I used that a lot and was convinced it really did help—until this time!

After the casts were off, it was still summer, and I could not wait to get my feet wet in the swimming pool. I still had to use crutches, but at the edge of the pool, those were thrown down, and I jumped into the water! It felt so good after nine weeks of being in casts!

I was finally able to lead Shirley to Christ, but she still lived her way. The only thing I could do was to let go and let God take care of her His way and in His time.

In my junior year, I went to a dinner they had for us for the junior-senior prom. It really was not all that great. That was also the year my grandpa was moved into Western Prairie Care Home. I was taking a class to learn guitar, but I had too much NF related coordination problems, so I quit the guitar lessons. Then I got a job at the care home.

I took the CNA class and passed the first time. I worked from 1:00 p.m. to 9:00 p.m. After I graduated, I worked all shifts. Later I changed to the 11:00 p.m. to 7:00 a.m. shift to see if I could keep from hurting my back, but I severely sprained it helping a resident to the bedside commode. She lost her balance, and I accidentally dropped her on the floor. The next day I went and had my back x-rayed, and it was found it had been severely sprained, so I was told it would be a good idea for me not to do that sort of work. I didn't realize that bone problems were a part of NF and that I shouldn't be doing work that put heavy strains on my back, legs, and feet.

I didn't have many noticeable tumors on my face until after I got out of high school; then they began to appear around the edges of my nostrils, around my eyes, and on my chin. They were very small for several years, but they kept growing imperceptibly and relentlessly. Today I have quite a lot of tumors on my face but not nearly as many as on other areas of my body. I pray that the ones on my eyelids don't get big enough to interfere with my vision! I have friends with NF whose faces make mine look smooth! But they do not have some of my problems that are worse than the bumps.

The fact that there weren't any bumps noticeable on my face in my senior pictures was a big relief to me. I was really happy and thankful about it, because those senior pictures seem to follow you throughout life!

I graduated in 1980 and even went to the senior prom, a memory I'd rather not have. I actually had a date, but I would not go to the dance. I did not know how to dance and didn't want people making fun of me for trying. We went to a church party, and the guys went downstairs while the girls stayed upstairs. This was my first date in my life, as most of the boys looked at me and only saw the tumors; they watched me and only saw that I was uncoordinated and walked funny. I feel sad that this date is a bad memory.

My graduation just meant that I was out of high school. At our graduation ceremony, we walked in pairs, and I walked with Shirley.

Wayne, the guy I had the prom date with, begged me to go to the drive-in movie with him the night after my sister got married. I did not want to go but did, just to shut him up. He had given me two lamps for graduation. When we went to the movie, it was a double feature; the first one was good, but the second one was not. He kept saying I was too young and should not be seeing that movie.

He proposed to me, and I said, "No way, we don't even know each other, and I don't love you." Even though I wanted to date, I wouldn't consider marriage at that age, to someone I didn't know and who didn't understand what I was facing with the NF.

When he took me home, he was angry about my answer, and to make sure he beat me into the house, he pushed me off the porch, ran inside, and took back the lamps he had given me. I found out he had been dating Shirley the nights I worked at the care home, so I knew I had made the right decision concerning him!

I really regret now that I wasn't more serious about my studies while I was in school. The fact that I have NF made school hard and not a lot of fun because of my dyslexia and poor coordination and the continual taunts of my classmates; but if I had been more serious about it, college might have been easier for me.

In 1981, I decided to enroll in Seward County Community College in Liberal, Kansas. I wanted to be a physical therapist, but the guy who taught that was a bully kind of man who would explode into profanity and act like we were idiots if we didn't understand something or asked him to explain it again. Then I tried the nursing program but could not pass the math required for it.

I lived in the dorm at SCCC and also worked at the nursing home there in Liberal. Over Christmas break, none of us could stay in the dorms, and I had to be in Liberal for my job. My mom's high school classmate and friend, Roberta Hartshorn, lived there, and she kindly let me stay at her house during the break. When Mom thanked her for this kindness, Roberta said, "She sure wasn't any trouble!"

She asked Mom a lot of questions about NF, and Mom was glad to be able to educate her about this condition. She hadn't seen me for probably ten years, since I was a small child, and was shocked to see the difference in my appearance. My family was with me all the time, so they didn't notice the differences so much; but when someone saw me who hadn't been around me, the difference was remarkable to them.

I changed my major to special education and then transferred to Fort Hays State University in Hays. When I transferred, math again became a subject required for my major. That was not good, because algebra was not my strong point. I could not pass it, and my advisor told me I needed to be in a junior college where it would be easier on me. I took college algebra three times but never passed. My dyslexia just made it impossible. I wanted to work with children who had learning or physical disabilities, because I knew I could relate to them and help them do better and feel better about themselves. I still regret that I was unable to do that. I understand how it feels to be different from others.

I had moved away from Boise City when I was ready to start seventh grade and didn't see many people from there for at least six years. I went to Boise City a couple of years after I graduated from high school to help my dad in the greenhouse he ran, and while there, some of my former teachers from school came in.

They recognized me and we visited, but I could tell they were shocked at how much I had changed. Later, Dad told me they asked him what was going on, and he explained that the NF was continuing its course and causing me more problems all the time. Nobody expected the NF to change the whole course of my life!

WORKING AS A NANNY

Beth had accumulated over $10,000 in student loan debt by the time she left college. She wanted to pay it off as quickly as she could, so after leaving South Hutchinson, she got in touch with a family in Dallas who needed a caregiver for their fourteen-year-old son. Ryan had been born with an incomplete brain stem, and he couldn't walk unassisted nor talk very plainly. His older sister had recently passed away from the same condition. Beth and Ryan got along well, but once, when taking him for a walk, she forgot to lock the wheels on his wheelchair, and he rolled off a small step and fell on his face. Beth was scared and upset because she thought she had hurt Ryan, but he was all right. She remembers being more upset than his mom, who kept trying to reassure Beth he was okay.

While in Dallas, Beth had her first opportunity to go to an NF support group meeting. There, for the very first time, she met others with NF, including a boy around her age named John Parker, who had had a cow bone grafted into his spine in the first such surgery. She became good friends with John's mother, June, who picked her up and took her to the support group meetings. She also met a little boy, a toddler, who was soon to have an eye removed because of NF.

When she called me after that first meeting, I asked her how she felt now that she had met others with NF. She said, "Well, Mom, I don't feel so alone any more, but I just wish there were something I could do to help all these people!" She felt especially sorry for the toddler boy who had to have the eye removed. He had massive NF tumors completely covering the eye and most of that side of his face.

Beth worked with Ryan and got him to eat foods he had previously refused, such as salads. He was allergic to wheat and many other things. She would also take him to the toilet and managed to get him trained—a huge accomplishment!

I visited her once while she was there and found Ryan to be fascinating. While he was quite limited, he also seemed bright. When he did something good, he was rewarded with ten M&Ms. He would count them, saying each number out loud (since I knew what he was doing, I understood him) then eat one. Again, count each one, eat another, and count again, and so on until the last one was gone. He had a board with words written on it, and if he couldn't make himself understood, he would grab the board, find the word, and jab it with his finger impatiently to get you to understand what he was saying.

Beth stayed at that job for over three years, and during that time, she paid off all of her student loans. I was very proud of her for that. While she lived in Dallas, her attendance at the NF support group meetings were an encouragement to her, and she got to go to several meetings where they had doctors and researchers who taught them more about the disorder. They encouraged them to go to a Neurologist for tests so that a baseline could be established with which to compare future changes in their health.

I was privileged to visit Beth in Dallas and go to a fundraiser with her. They were selling chances to win a beautiful palomino horse, and Beth told me she wished she could win him. Of course, she had no place to keep a horse and knew it wasn't possible.

Ryan's uncle had two little kids, and he began to leave them with Beth as she cared for Ryan. She thought he should pay her for taking care of them, but he expected her to do it for nothing because he was her employer's brother.

When she was ready to leave that job with Ryan, June told Beth that she needed to go home and live with her parents. Beth said, "No, I don't. I don't want to live with my parents."

June told her she couldn't live by herself; she needed us to take care of her because of the NF and the problems it might cause her in the future. Beth said, "No, I don't! My mom always told me I can do anything I want to do!"

When Beth told me about this conversation, I thought, *Well, good! She was listening!*

In 1986 Beth was offered a nanny job in Reston, Virginia. Her charges were a five-year-old boy named Matt and a four-year-old girl named Liz. The kids responded well to Beth from the start and never acted as if they noticed she looked any different from others. She enjoyed this job a lot. She also worked in a daycare part time after Liz started kindergarten.

Beth really liked the area because of the natural beauty of the trees and water and the nice climate. She learned to get around on the bus and the subway, enabling her to take the kids to the zoo, the wildlife park, where they rode an elephant, and to the pool. They also enjoyed the shopping center down the road.

There were many girls in that area working as nannies, and they would get together once in a while. They made a couple of short trips together too. It's always good to have friends.

She took a part-time job at a daycare when both kids were in school. Later, it was arranged for them to also come to after-school care, so she did both jobs. At that time, she was still walking, but her gait was strange. None of us realized the reason was that the NF was steadily progressing. Most people just thought she was awkward and uncoordinated and, sadly, that she might be a bit retarded. This was unfair and untrue, but those old stereotypes are hard to erase from people's minds.

Nanny Plus Daycare
—Beth—

In the daycare, I was assigned first to work with the three-year-olds and the kitchen part time. Later, I worked with the infants. I liked that the best because I got to see them grow into individuals, each with their own personality. In the two years I worked there,

I got attached to each child, and it was hard to see them move to a different class. I got attached to one child named Cody, and he liked me too.

I got along well with the two children for whom I was a nanny, and it was really hard to leave when the time came. I was with this family for several years. The incident that led to my being let go was that I had a really bad headache one day; I took something for it and fell asleep. While I slept, Matt put a plastic toy on the bulb of a lamp, where it melted. The mom didn't know anything about NF or that headaches are often another problem caused by it, so she didn't ask me why I was napping when she came home and smelled it. She got really upset, saying it could have started a fire and burned down the house.

EMOTIONS AND NF

When small children started staring at her, Beth wasn't offended, as she knew it was just normal curiosity. But if they kept staring too long, she told them to take a picture; it would last longer.

A girl of about fourteen followed Beth all around at an arts and crafts show, staring at her. Finally, she got up enough courage to ask Beth what was wrong. Beth kindly explained NF to her, assuring her that it was not "catching." That satisfied the girl, and she walked away.

Usually, parents or older siblings will tell kids that it's not nice to stare at people. When adults openly stare at her, it really bothers Beth; she would much rather they approach her and ask about her condition.

At a water park, a boy of nine or ten kept following Beth around for a long time, staring at her, and finally asked her what was wrong. Feeling tired of being stared at and treated like a freak, she told him, "I have neurofibromatosis, and if you get too close, it will jump on you!" His eyes got huge, and he ran away as fast as he could go! She said she was feeling ornery that day.

Having NF has made Beth more compassionate and careful not to stare at others who were different. If she has a chance, she will engage them in conversation.

One little girl asked Beth, "What are those things on you?"

Beth answered, "I was told they are angel kisses."

"Then why are some of them red?"

"Uh…I guess some of them must have been wearing lipstick!"

As more and more NF nodules appeared, Beth thought, *These things make me look yucky. How am I ever going to catch a man, looking like this?* In 1981, the movie *Elephant Man* came out, and she feared she would wind up looking like that, and she wondered what circus would hire her to be in their freak show. It was a huge relief to learn later that the Elephant Man, John Merrick, suffered from a condition called Proteus syndrome, and not from NF.

Just weeks ago, the family gathered to celebrate the Resurrection of Jesus. Lexi, her three-and-a-half-year-old great-niece, looked Beth over and asked, "Why do you have bubbles on you? Can you pop them?"

Beth got a chuckle out of this innocent question. She said some of the neurofibromas do look like little bubbles; they are even shiny!

Beth met a lady about her age over in Johnson. She had NF but was married and had children. Her NF was causing her lots of problems, and Beth said it was so comforting to be able to talk with someone who really understood how it is to live with NF. Later, she heard that lady and her husband were divorced and had moved away, and Beth was sorry to lose contact with an understanding friend.

VISITING BETH IN VIRGINIA

D arrel had found Beth a reliable used car, and in order for her to have it in Virginia, she flew home for a visit. While at home, she told me that Elaine was letting her go soon after my visit, which had been planned for months. Then she and I drove the car to Virginia. When I got to Reston and met Elaine, her reaction was, "You're Beth's mother? But—you're so pre...Oh! I'm sorry, Beth!"

By this, I knew she thought Beth looked bad and fully expected that I would also have NF. This is a misconception people sometimes have—that NF is always hereditary. It was a hurtful comment, but she hadn't intended any offense, and none was taken. But I was happy her kids hadn't seemed to notice or care about Beth's appearance.

After visiting with her there for a while, I flew home. As a special treat and gift for both my birthday and Elaine's, Beth bought the three of us tickets to see *The Phantom of the Opera* at the Kennedy Center in Washington, DC. She purchased those tickets before Elaine let her go, so of course she didn't back out of the deal. We did go; it was a fantastic live play, with wonderful special effects. It is a special memory of Beth's gift of love whenever I think of that evening.

Fun Times and Challenges
—Beth—

In 1987 I took a scuba diving class in Virginia and got all of it completed except the open-water tests. I was going home to Kansas for a visit and was able to take the open water at Lake Meredith, near Amarillo.

After I got my open-water scuba certification—not an easy accomplishment with my NF problems—I went to Cozumel, Mexico, with Mom and Darrel. They were concerned because I was such a new diver, so they hired a young dive master just to stay with me. I liked that! He was handsome and considerate and kind, and we had a really good time diving. The fish and the corals are so beautiful, the water so warm and clear, I think it must be a little foretaste of heaven! And at the end of the dive, my dive master lifted the heavy gear back onto the boat for me.

Once I even got to go parasailing! That was really fun! The guys on the boat dipped me in the water as I was coming down, thinking it would scare me, but I thought it was fun! Sometimes people are extra kind to me because they understand I have a problem that is not in my control. Kindness is always appreciated!

In the following years, I got to go to Roatan, Honduras, five times on dive trips with Mom and Darrel. I am so thankful to have had those experiences while I was still able to walk.

On one trip, a fellow Mom and Darrel knew there invited the three of us for a sail on his boat, the *Honky Tonk*. It was a beautiful evening just about dusk, the water was smooth as glass and the weather perfect. And the captain even let me steer the boat for a while! What a special memory that is.

On the last trip I was on to Roatan, our eye doctor, Greg Copeland, his wife, Karen, and their daughter were with us. We all enjoyed diving, and Karen and Mom kept an eye on me because I was no longer a strong swimmer, especially while wearing heavy scuba gear. People at the resort treated me well and helped me carry the heavy gear and air tanks, but the scariest challenge was to come after we boarded the plane to fly home.

A SCARY EXPERIENCE!

This scene is burned into my memory. We had boarded the plane to come home from Roatan, Honduras, and I was settling into my seat when I heard Beth's panicked voice.

"Mom! Come up here!" She was sitting several rows ahead of us, and the flight attendant was standing there beside her. When I got there, Beth said, almost in tears, "Tell her that I'm not contagious! She wants to throw me off the plane!"

I explained NF to the girl, but she wanted to know if we had a doctor with us who could confirm that it wasn't contagious. In my distress, I didn't think to ask Dr. Copeland to come up there; he's not an MD, but he's a doctor nonetheless and would have given them a good story for Beth.

Anyway, the flight attendant wasn't satisfied, so she told me I would have to go to the cockpit and explain NF to the pilots! So once again, I explained that the condition was not contagious, saying, "I'm her mother, and I've been around her all her life. Do I look like I have caught anything from her?"

The pilots didn't give me any problem; I really think it was just that the flight attendant was scared. When I went back and told Dr. Copeland, he said he sure wished I'd called him; he would have fixed it for us.

A lady who had been at the same dive resort as us felt so badly for Beth about this incident that she gave her a beautiful, little gold manta ray pendant. That was such a sweet gesture.

Another time, when Beth went to the swimming pool, they weren't going to let her swim because they thought others might catch NF from her.

More Work
—Beth—

After leaving the nanny position, I stayed at the daycare. I lived with another family, but their child was older and in school all day. I lived there mostly because they let me; they sort of took advantage of me, wanting me to always stay with the boy and just assuming I would do it out of the goodness of my heart. They moved to another house, and my room was just bigger than a full-size bed. I was paying rent, but it became too costly to live there.

I left there and took another nanny position, again with a boy and a girl. I was not
driving because I'd had an accident and
totaled my car. I was not injured, and if I had
been near home, Darrel probably could have
gotten the car fixed, but that was the end
of my driving in Virginia. I really couldn't
take Jake and Samantha anywhere except
the small play park almost in their back-
yard. I was there for a few months and was
let go because I almost stepped on crawling
Samantha, whom I didn't see. I said, "Damn
it," and her mom heard me and thought I'd
said it to Sam, not out of frustration. She
thought I was swearing at her daughter,
which I would never do.

As I was going about my life, making my
own living and dealing with things in gen-
eral, the NF tumors continued to multiply.
They became so numerous on my back that
a finger could not be touched there without
touching at least two or more of the bumps.
I had some back problems and some headaches, but I just took something like Tylenol
and went on about my business. I was used
to pain, anyway. And I had no idea they were
to get so much worse. Now I would give anything to go back to the abilities I had earlier
in life, even at the time I lived in Virginia.

During the time I was in Reston, I was
around several people who used really bad
language. Before I realized what was happening, I heard this kind of stuff coming

out of my mouth too. I was upset about it; I didn't want to be a potty mouth! I had found a church I really liked and was attending it. One Sunday, I asked them to pray for me that I would not use bad language anymore. They prayed for me, and after that, God reminded me every time something bad started to come out of my mouth; and before long, no more swearing! God is so good!

I moved back to Kansas, then back to Dallas to take care of the four-year-old daughter of a longtime friend, Mary. Monica and I got along great. She loved to walk, and we went lots of places together: fishing, to Taco Tico to eat, to the corner store, etc. We had good times together. I stayed there with them about a year and then I moved back to Kansas and went to work for High Plains Educational Co-op. They sent me to Johnson, Kansas, to work as a parapro-fessional for a thirteen-year-old student with autism.

This proved to be very challenging. The student was hard to handle and had the strength of an elephant. He did not talk, but he made a lot of noise, banged his hands on his head, and screamed. He was not toilet-trained, really, and there was not a good place to take him where people did not come in. We used the girls' locker room and the bathroom that the senior citizens used.

One day while in the bathroom, he got underneath the paper towel holder and began to bang his head against it, jumping up and down, and banging his face on it too. I tried to pull him away, but he was too strong, and he screamed and hit at me. This incident caused bruises, and his mother accused me of abusing him, so my position changed again. I went to Big Bow, Kansas, to the elementary school and to Johnson Elementary. In those schools, I had several students who needed help with various subjects. This position ended with the end of the school year. This was probably just as well, because by this time my walking was getting worse and worse. I now had tumors everywhere on my body but not yet too many on my face.

I have always related well with children, and each family I worked for gave me good references when I left. Some of the children I cared for still call me today.

THE ENEMY WITHIN

Beth was a determined girl; no matter how many problems she ran into or how often she had to find another job, she kept on trying. For one who had as many problems physically as she had, I felt she was such a strong person, never giving up. In spite of her increasing problems with strength and coordination and the attending pain of headaches, backaches and pains in her arms, hands and legs, she kept on keeping on. She was determined to support herself and not have to depend on us. It was hard watching her those years but also gratifying to know that her faith remained strong and she trusted God to help her. Wherever she lived, she found a church to attend, and her attitude was one of continual optimism.

All the years Beth was working, moving around the country, and taking care of kids, the NF was relentlessly attacking her body in ways we couldn't see or know. We did notice some changes in her walking, her posture, and her feet, but we just blindly hoped that it would continue to be mainly a cosmetic problem. How little we knew! During these years, we did take her to various doctors: dermatologists, neurologists, endocrinologist, nutritionists, bone and joint orthopedics. She had so many tests done—bone scans, brain scans, many MRIs, CT scans, nerve conduction studies, spinal tap, psychological exams, even a test where they put her on a table that spun her around, then she had to stand and try to walk then lie down flat—but her condition continued to worsen. She endured all these painful tests with stoicism and good humor and hoped along with us for them to find some way to help her, or if not to help, at least slow or stop the progression of NF on her body.

She was seeing a wonderful doctor in Amarillo, an endocrinologist, Dr. Stephen Usala. He said he wished she could move there so he could better care for her and that he would take care of her free if she couldn't afford to pay. I never thought I would meet such a caring physician.

Dr. Usala found a hard little nodule in Beth's thyroid, and he was very concerned that it may be cancerous. He did tests repeatedly, sent them off to the best experts he knew, and only after they assured him it was an NF nodule did he accept that it wasn't cancer. The time came when he could do nothing further to help Beth, but his kindness will never be forgotten.

Beth's next job was caring for a three-year-old child and infant twins at Hugoton, whose mother had died of cancer right after the twins' birth. She found it hard to carry two babies around, and the dad didn't have a double stroller. The dad remarried before long. Beth was there about six months.

She returned to Ulysses, where she worked a series of jobs: school bus aid (helping handicapped kids on and off the bus), working at McDonalds, and the job as a paraprofessional with High Plains Educational Co-op.

SEABOARD FARMS

—Beth—

By October of 1995, Seaboard Farms had established pig farms all over our area. They paid good wages, so I applied there and was hired as a production worker. I was thirty-five years old at this time.

The farm I was assigned to was a genetic one, near Syracuse, Kansas. That was a fifty-mile trip each way, but I was thankful not to have to drive it myself, as they had a company vehicle that was driven by an employee who lived in Ulysses, and the other employees from Ulysses could ride along.

The hours of work were supposed to be from 7:00 a.m. to 4:00 p.m., but I never got to leave before 10:00 p.m. The work I did was heavy and hard. I enjoyed working with the piglets but not having to do the things required to do to them that caused them pain. I had to nip off the pigs' teeth with a cutter, snip off half the length of their tails, castrate the males, and give them all shots. This work put a heavy strain on my hands and was almost more than I could do. By now my hands had so many tumors they appeared to be deformed, and I no longer had as much strength in them. Fine muscle coordination had always been a problem for me, and this work made it worse.

I worked at Farm 1 for nine months. My boss was Lori Jacobson, with whom I became good friends. Lori has a sister with handicaps, so she was kind and understanding to me and also a lot of fun to be with. One day Lori confronted me and asked, "What are you doing to the pigs in your four rooms?"

Startled, I asked, "Why?"

Lori responded, "Because they do better, are healthier, and gain weight faster than any other pigs on the farm!"

Relieved, I said, "Oh, that! Well, I just sing to them, and before I set them down, I give them a kiss and apologize to them for having to hurt them!"

In June of 1996, I was transferred to another farm. It was closer to home, and I drove myself to and from work. I had several different bosses, but Lori was the best by far. She was transferred too and became the manager of that farm, and she was the only one who ever showed she cared or trusted me.

Almost every woman and girl I worked with had children. They were visiting at lunch about their kids and asked me, "Beth, how many kids do you have?" I answered, "I'm not married." They said, "So? How many kids do you have?" I explained that I was taught that you get married first, then you have children, and they wondered what planet I was from!

After Lori left, I had a lot of problems with the managers who followed her. I went out of my way to be a good worker, going in early and going to the barns early, but they never told me I was doing well; all I ever heard was negative remarks. I truly believed I was doing more than mediocre, but the way I was talked to and treated proved me wrong. I really felt I was being judged not by the quality or quantity of the work I did but by my appearance.

A disease swept through the whole farm that caused the mother sows' milk to curdle in the piglets' stomachs. We were told the only way to get rid of it was to destroy all the piglets and then they ground them up and fed them back to the sows. I thought this was horrible, and I didn't want to kill the piglets. But I had to do it.

The way it was done was to pick up the babies by their hind legs and slam their heads onto the concrete floor. I killed 300 pigs in one day, and then I went home and cried. I told Mom I felt like a murderer of innocent piglets; they could not hurt me, yet I slaughtered them.

One job that all of us in that particular position did each week was to carry in fifty-pound bags of powdered milk. This was not a short distance, and the cart we were told to use was one meant for feed. It was deep and only held six bags at a time. It was hard to unload, and the bags were heavy and hard to carry, because my back, legs, and arms were no longer as strong because of the NF. I probably shouldn't have worked there, but I wanted to support myself so I did what I had to do.

One job I did that brought the most complaints from the bosses was the way I power washed. Each room in the two barns in the farrowing department had to be power washed five days a week. There were sixteen rooms and two barns, so there were eight rooms in each barn. There were forty-eight sows in each room; every week, one room's pigs were weaned and the piglets sent to a nursery. Every crate had to be cleaned and every speck of dirt and waste washed away.

This proved to be heavy and hard work and it seemed like I was always picked to do it. This took most of the day, and it had to pass inspection by the in-charge person. There was a handle you held with a trigger that had to be squeezed to allow the water to spray out. Holding the trigger was not that simple; the half of the room was not small, and holding pressure on it for hours caused lots of pain in my hands.

I began having pain in both hands. Processing the litters was tedious, as I had to hold the piglet with one hand while I did the necessary things with the other. That plus the power washing caused me tremendous pain, which was diagnosed as bilateral carpal tunnel syndrome. I was given splints to wear until I could have surgery and put on light duty. You can imagine how fast those splints got filthy!

Light duty consisted of cleaning the office, doing all the laundry (all employees were required to shower in each morning and change into company clothing, and then shower and change back into their own clothing after clocking out), washing dishes in the break room, and cleaning up after the other employees. The workers were always taking my hand splints and hiding them while I was washing dishes or doing other things for which I had to remove them.

During this time, I learned that cleaning up after the pigs was easier than cleaning up after the human pigs. They went out of their way to make messes for me to clean, just because they didn't have to clean up after themselves. They also squeezed into underwear several sizes too small and ruined them, stole packages of new socks, and overloaded the washer and dryer, causing the company to have to replace them every few months.

Since my left hand was the worst, I had the surgery on it first and stayed on light duty until the doctor dismissed me. It took a long time before my hands could be used in that way again.

I continued working there and tolerated the other employees who treated me like garbage.

On March 11, 1997, as I was driving home from work, I was involved in a really bad car accident. I had the right of way, I was on the highway, and I never saw the car that hit me, which was crossing the highway from an unpaved country road. The driver was going 70 miles per hour and ran a stop sign, hitting my car in the driver's door. The impact sent my car airborne for 200 feet, where it landed in a freshly plowed and irrigated field. Thank God I had on my seatbelt; otherwise, I would probably have been thrown from the car and maybe killed.

I was knocked unconscious, and the other driver opened the passenger door, unfastened my seatbelt, and dragged me over the center console and out of the car. He dragged me right out of my shoes, through the mud, and draped me over an irrigation pipe.

A lady who lived near the accident scene saw the wreck and called 911. An ambulance from Johnson, Kansas, came, and they took me to the hospital in Johnson. The nurse on the ambulance was someone I had known for years, and she was surprised I recognized her, because I hadn't seen her for a long time and I had been unconscious.

I was asked whom they should call, and I gave them my mom's name and number.

When I answered the phone on the afternoon of March 11, 1997, I didn't recognize the caller's voice. He asked, "Is Beth Brandt your mother?"

I answered, "Hardly. She is my daughter."

He was surprised at my answer, for whatever reason, and asked, "Are you sure?"

When I assured him I was, indeed, Beth's mom, he told me she had been in an accident. I asked if she was hurt, and where was she, and should I come. He was reluctant to say what her injuries were, but he said I probably should come. I quickly found my husband, and we headed to Johnson to the hospital.

When we got there, Beth was very relieved to see us. She was in a great deal of pain, her left leg was encased in a blue blow-up splint to hold it in place, and we were told her femur was broken, but they didn't think she had any other injuries. However, they wanted to transport her to Garden City, where better facilities were available. I requested to ride in the ambulance with her.

I was jolted back to the present by our arrival in the ambulance at St. Catherine's Hospital in Garden City. Would Beth be all right? Did she have other injuries not yet detected? They quickly whisked her away on a gurney for tests, and I was left standing alone in the hallway. Darrel would be arriving soon, so I looked for a quiet place in the waiting room and tried to calm my mind and concentrate on praying for Beth. This was not the first time I had kept vigil over her in a hospital, and it would not be the last.

A Really Rough Ambulance Ride
—Beth—

When my mom got to the emergency room in Johnson, she asked why I was covered in mud, and they told her about the other driver dragging me. They had to cut my clothes off me, ruining my favorite green T-shirt, in order to assess my injuries. I was taken to Garden City by ambulance, and it was a long, bumpy, and very uncomfortable ride.

In Garden City, they discovered my injuries included the broken femur, plus my pelvis was broken in two places. They put me in a regular room, rigged my leg up with traction, and thought one of their orthopedic doctors could fix my leg and then I could go home.

Several people from our church came and prayed for me. After three days I was getting really sick and was moved into intensive care, where they found I had blood clots in my lung that were life threatening. We have always wondered if the rough ambulance ride contributed to this.

My friend, Mindi, from college days, lived in Holcomb, only a few miles from Garden City, and she had been to visit me in the hospital the second day I was there. She came back the afternoon I was moved to intensive care, went to my room, and found it empty, and she panicked! When she finally spotted my mom in the hall, she ran to her with tears streaming down her face and asked, "Where is Beth? Did something happen?"

Poor Mindi! She was so relieved to learn I was still alive.

On the evening of Friday, March 14, I was flown by Life Watch to St. Francis Hospital in Wichita, the same hospital where I had had my previous surgeries back when I was in school. I told Mom that when I finally got to ride in a small plane, I couldn't see out the window, and I didn't even get a package of peanuts to eat!

I was placed in ICU, where I stayed for ten days. I had blood clots in my lungs, so I had a nose tube, heart monitors, IVs, and various other tubes. I was in bad shape, so when the nurses and doctors talked to my mom, they tried to hide how bad I was from me by not letting me hear or see them when they spoke to my mom in my presence. But they really could not keep it from me because I was over the age of eighteen.

The first thing they did to stabilize my leg was to put me in traction to hold the bone in place until they could go in and insert a titanium rod in it. The traction was screwed into my leg bones in the lower leg.

On Saturday, March 15, I had two procedures done. One was putting the screws in my left leg, and the other was putting in a Greenfield filter to catch blood clots before any more could enter my lungs. They had to insert two, because the first one didn't open properly. A few days later, I went back into surgery to have the rod inserted into the center of the femur to hold it in place while it healed.

I remember Mom putting shamrock stickers on my leg on St. Patrick's Day. She did whatever she could to lighten the mood and make me smile.

I needed a PICC so they could do blood draws from it instead of having to stick me each time. This had to be done precisely right and x-rayed when done to check for placement. The doctor who was doing it didn't get it right the first time, and he felt awful about it. Nor was it right on the second try.

He was sweating and dreading trying it again, really distressed to have to hurt me again. My mom stepped over to him, laid her hand on his shoulder, and prayed for him that it would go perfectly this time and that he wouldn't feel nervous about it and that God would bless him for being compassionate. He thanked her, took a deep breath and exhaled, then tried again, and this time got it perfectly. God is so good! He answered Mom's prayer and guided the doctor's hands on that third try.

The first time they got me out of bed after surgery, I looked as bad as I felt. I also had my first solid food there, a great big hamburger that I could not finish.

While I was still in ICU, I started running a fever, so they wouldn't let me have any covers, not even a sheet, and I was so cold. They were giving me morphine for the pain, and it caused me to have nightmares. I was really happy when Mom and Bonnie walked into my room each morning and I returned to reality; even though reality wasn't exactly fun at that point.

A FRIEND IN A TIME OF NEED

Our wonderful friends, Eugene and Bonnie Swindler, had come to Wichita along with Darrel, and Bonnie decided to stay with me. She was such a blessing from God, encouraging me, doing my hair for me, praying with me, just being everything one could ask in a friend. When we would go into Beth's room, Beth would ask us to sing to her, and we sang many choruses that we sang in church. These songs comforted Beth and helped her to sleep.

> For you are my hope, O Lord God. You are my trust from my youth. By You I have been upheld from my youth, You are He who took me out of my mother's womb. My praise shall be continually of You.
>
> Psalm 71:5-6 (NIV)

Even in times of greatest stress and pain, Beth amazed us by maintaining a sense of humor. She would try to have a joke ready with which to greet us each morning. She kept our spirits up probably more than we did hers! She told me later that because she knew Jesus, she wasn't worried about dying, because that would mean she got to go to heaven sooner, and how could that be bad?

There were many crises during this hospitalization. It seemed there was a new one almost every day. I don't even recall all of them now, but some were: they thought her kidneys had shut down; she developed an infection that caused her fever to spike; the first Greenfield filter they put in failed to open, and several other things. But the presence of the Lord was with us in such a special way that even though it hurt to see Beth suffering, still I had a peace in my heart the whole time, remembering what the Word says, "Thou wilt keep him in perfect peace, whose mind is stayed on thee, because he trusteth in thee" (Isaiah 26:3, KJV).

We were trusting in the Lord; we knew only He could bring Beth through this ordeal. She was very close to death at several points, but at each crisis, Bonnie and I would find a quiet corner and talk to God about what was happening. We felt assured Beth would be okay and that God still had plans for her life.

There were other families sharing the ICU waiting room, and Bonnie and I had the opportunity to pray with several of them for their loved ones. It helps to help others when you have needs, for what we sow into others' lives comes back into our own.

Bonnie and I were blessed to be able to stay at the Perdue House not far from the hospital. This was similar to a Ronald McDonald House, except the patients did not have to be children for the families to stay there. This was such a great blessing to be able to talk to others, make meals in the kitchen, and have a home-like atmosphere. It was so much better than having to stay in a motel room, and much less costly.

Beth's main nurse in the ICU was really a cranky gal. In fact, when our beloved pastor, Bill Marquardt, and his wife, Tata, came to see Beth, Tata, who is a nurse herself, said, "Get another nurse!" This was after the cranky nurse ran us out of Beth's room three times while Pastor Bill was praying for her. But Bonnie and I told her we didn't want another nurse; this one really knew her stuff, and we were praying for her attitude to change and that God would change her heart. We were careful to be extra kind and polite to her and always give her a big smile and express appreciation for the good care she was giving Beth.

One night Beth was singing "The Joy of the Lord Is My Strength" while this nurse was in her room, and the nurse thought she was nuts!

When you ask God for things that are His will, He answers, and sometimes very quickly! Cranky nurse, within a few days, went from running us out of Beth's room to allowing us extra time and extra visits, ordering up food for me, and returning our smiles. Before we left there, I went to the hospital gift shop and bought the nurse a little thank-you gift. Whenever I think of her, I still pray for her. She blessed our lives.

An amusing incident with this nurse was the story she told us when she brought Beth one of those plastic instruments you suck on to exercise your lungs. It has a ball in it that is supposed to rise as you inhale. She told us she handed one to a male patient one day and told him to suck as hard as he could. He tried, but the ball never budged. She told him to try harder; he did, with still no movement by the ball. So she yelled at him, saying he wasn't even trying!

He shoved the thing at her and said, "You do it!"

So she sanitized the tube and tried until her eyeballs nearly popped, she said, and that ball did not move one iota. Then she looked really closely at it and discovered the ball was actually glued to the bottom! She said that since that incident, she always turns the thing upside down or shakes it to be sure the ball is loose!

When Beth was able to go to physical therapy, her therapist was a jolly black man whose nickname was "Chop." We asked about that, and he said it was because he loved karate. Beth was now using a walker, and Chop taught her the way to remember how to go up and down steps. "Good people go to heaven; bad people go to hell," he said. This was to help her remember to go *up* on the good leg and *down* on the bad leg.

After ten days in ICU, Beth was moved to a regular room upstairs. Her ICU nurse (cranky) took her upstairs herself. She kept saying, "I don't know why I'm doing this. I never did it before or ever wanted to, but for some reason you are different."

Bonnie and I looked at each other and smiled, and I winked. We knew why!

GOING HOME

—Beth—

They were going to put me in the room with another woman, but I had a CDIF infection they would rather I not share, so I was put in a private room. I was really happy about that, as I didn't feel up to having a roommate.

I got to go home two days before Easter. When we called Darrel, he started out right away for Wichita, and when he arrived after the four-hour drive, we still had to wait almost three hours for them to get my discharge papers done so I could leave! When I left, I was put in the backseat, but it was very uncomfortable, so when we stopped to eat, Mom put me in the front seat, which she moved all the way back and reclined for me. This was much more comfortable. Mom rode in the backseat, and Darrel drove. Bonnie had gone home after I got out of ICU.

I wanted to go to church on Easter, so Mom and Darrel took me. Pastor Bill said from the pulpit, "Well! There's Beth, back from the dead!" It was wonderful to see him and the rest of my church family. They had been praying faithfully for me all the time.

Once I got home, my dog Sindee would not leave me. I hadn't seen her since my accident, and she missed me as much as I missed her. I moved back in with Mom and Darrel, since I had been living in the dome house and could not climb the spiral staircase to the bedroom.

A few days after I came home, I was in a great deal of pain. I was trying to get to sleep but hurt too much. I felt a sweet presence come into the room, and I felt myself gently picked up, wrapped in something soft, and held suspended above the bed. The pain left, and I was able to sleep through the night. After that, when I had trouble sleeping, I'd be reminded of this experience and knew that I was safe in the arms of my Savior. I really believe this was an angelic visitation, sent to me in my time of need to reassure me of God's love.

Our church was Faith Fellowship and our pastor, Bill Marquardt, was a wonderful man of God. When I came home, he asked both Mom and me to talk about everything we had been through. We did, and I was shy about using a microphone but wish I had, as it was recorded, but my voice wasn't audible on the cassette. Mom was telling about me not breathing properly, and she had to keep reminding me, "Breathe, Beth!"

Pastor Bill looked at me with a mischievous grin and said, "Well, she *is* blonde!"

We shared about the goodness of God and His mercy through the whole ordeal. He had asked Bonnie to share too, but she was unable to be there that evening.

Mom told our church family that we all need to have the Word in our hearts and not wait for a crisis and then run to find a Bible. And we can't always depend on having a pastor there, either, since sometimes he is not available in a crisis. We need to learn the Word, believe the Word, memorize it, and have it in our hearts; and then in times like that, the Word is what comes out of our mouths, not fear and unbelief. I thank God that Mom took me to church faithfully from the time I was born and that I had a lot of Word in my heart to sustain me through this and many other crisis times in my life.

Pastor Bill was not feeling at all well when he came to the hospital to visit me; and shortly after that, he was diagnosed with liver cancer. It hurt his entire congregation to see him suffer. He had taught us for years on the power of God to heal, and we prayed for him around the clock, but Bill went to the loving arms of Jesus in June 1997. It was only three weeks from diagnosis till death.

This devastated the church; each of us felt we had lost a precious member of our own family. His passing left a hole in the hearts of his flock, and nobody could be found to fill his shoes. It ultimately destroyed the church, as the shepherd was struck; then a wolf came in and scattered the sheep.

Back to Work Again

I was able to return to work, and I moved back into the geodesic dome. But things at work were not any better. I no longer used the walker when I was released to return to work. The company never did find a suitable person to be the manager. They had a series of managers, each no better than the one before. It made me miss my friend Lori all the more, as she had left to take another job.

I returned to full duty, doing all I had done before, without too many problems. New Year's Eve morning, I was in the barns doing my work when I tripped and fell on the grating on the floor. I split open a place on my left knee. I went and found one of the workers, who took me to the office and then found the farrowing leader. She told me to shower through, and then she drove me to the ER in Ulysses.

I had my car there, but she would not let me drive. In the ER, they put in an IV to ward off infection because of the environment I worked in. I had to have nine stitches, and I could not return to work until I saw the company nurse, so I did not work New Year's Day. On January 2, I drove to Rolla, Kansas, to see the company nurse. She said I was to stay out of the barns until my stitches were removed. I was to stay in the office and do light duty again just as before.

I was made to carry out all the trash, and it was not a short distance to the dumpsters. I asked the people who drove pickups if they would haul it to the dumpsters as they left. A few times they did, but then they told me it was too much work for them and not their job.

I had to drag the bags and hope they didn't break and spill the trash. I even tried putting them on the hood of my car and driving them to the Dumpsters, and this scratched the paint on my car. Many things I shouldn't have done and really wasn't able to do, I did by sheer determination because I felt I had no choice if I wanted to continue to support myself. I didn't want to whine or complain, so I gritted my teeth and kept going.

When she was about thirty-eight years old, Beth had noticed that whenever she received a trauma of any kind, such as a sow knocking a gate into her leg, it caused more

NF tumors to grow in that area. The wreck shook up her entire body, and the tumors began to grow inside her spinal column, exerting ever-increasing pressure on her spinal cord. This terrible, relentless enemy was slowly, inexorably robbing her of her mobility.

We had no idea, though, how quickly she would go downhill from this time. Even to those of us who saw her daily, her decline was dramatic! But she kept her chin up, her faith in God, and plodded on, doing daily the things required of her. Had I had any idea the toll that terrible job was taking on her poor body, I would not have allowed her to continue working there!

BETH'S FAMILY

During the years that Beth was still working and living near us, Darrel bought me a miniature dachshund, and Beth fell in love with her. I could see it was a match, so I gave her to Beth. She named her Sindee, and Sindee became her constant companion when she was home. She had her for several years, but then one morning when she went out the doggie door to tend to her business, Sindee just disappeared, and we never saw her again. She was heartbroken, as that dog was her family, providing unconditional love and lots of companionship for her. She also had a cat she named M&M, short for Motor Mouth, because she purred so loudly.

Her next dog was a Chihuahua puppy that she named Mieka, after a sweet little Chinese girl, a computer friend of mine. The name means "a tiny fish." Mieka was such a good little dog, and Beth loved her dearly. She would sing "You Are My Sunshine" to her, and Mieka would join in loudly!

After Beth became disabled but was still living at home, Mieka had one litter of four puppies, but only one survived. Beth said Mieka didn't win the title of Mother of the Year. The one that did survive, she named Miracle, and that puppy grew up on Beth's lap; she almost never left her, so of course she was really attached to her. These dogs were truly family to her!

But one day Miracle was outside, ran under a car, and was hit. We took her to the vet, and he kept her until the next afternoon, but the injuries were so severe that he recommended Beth let her go. So I took Beth out to the vet's, and she held and loved Miracle while the shot was administered, crying all the time. Later, she wrote the following poem:

Miracle

She stood upon the Rainbow Bridge, ready
    to cross the very wide ridge.
Sad and alone she felt that day, until she
    heard a gentle voice say,
"Welcome home, little one! You've been a
    blessing and your work is done.
Cross on over; come and play—you'll see
    your person again someday."
She crossed over, her legs were strong; and
    she knew in her heart that she was home.
She felt happy and her curly tail began
    to wag.

It was then she knew that her owner loved
   her and letting her go was the best thing
   to do.
She heard barking and looked around, she
   found her siblings she had never met,
And this new place would be fun yet.
Barking and running, she felt so free; there
   was grass and flowers and lots of trees.
So although she and her owner would be
   apart, she knew it would not be forever
And she could be happy and carefree.

She also wrote this:

Miracle

You touched my heart and life, my dear little
   one. The hardest thing was to let you go,
   but I know you are no longer in pain and
   I look forward to seeing you again.
Some people say that dogs are angels
   with tails.

After Beth had to move into the care home, Mieka came
to live with Darrel and me. I would take Mieka to visit,
and she always behaved very well. She would never bark
while there. She knew where Beth's room was, and she
would pull me along on the leash to Beth's room, jump
into her lap, and happily give her doggy kisses.

One day when I was visiting at the care home and had
Mieka along, there was a group of school children there
to entertain the residents. They were singing, and Mieka
joined in, loudly! I had to hustle her out of there, as she
was getting more attention than the kids!

When our neighbors moved, they gave their pet cockatoo, Ruffles, to Beth. Ruffles could speak several phrases, such as "Yeah, right," and "Hello, Ruffles"; she could wolf whistle and say other single words, so she was a lot of fun. The only drawback was that when the sun started going down, Ruffles began squawking—loudly! She would calm down if you covered her cage, but then she made cheesecloth out of any cover you used.

Ruffles was gentle and loved to snuggle into Beth's neck and have her scratch up under her neck feathers. She would come to those in the family she knew, and she made friends easily. In the summer, we moved her cage over to our garage, where we would keep the overhead door open in the daytime so she could have fresh air and sunshine.

While Ruffles was in the garage, she heard me several times as I stood at the bottom of the stairs and called, "Darrel! Hey, Darrel!" to him in his upstairs office, so I didn't have to climb up the stairs every time. Soon she learned to mimic my voice and would call, "Darrel! Hey, Darrel!" and he would go and open the door and not see me. It took a while to figure out it was Ruffles calling him.

When Darrel would be grilling, he took Ruffles out of her cage and let her walk around outdoors. She loved to sneak up on the cat and bite her tail!

When Beth's health and disability got so bad, she became unable to care for Ruffles because she couldn't walk, get the bird food and water, clean the cage, and give her the attention she needed. I really didn't want the mess in my house either. She remembered the kindness of one coworker at the last pig farm where she worked and who loved animals as much as she does. She let Ruffles go to live with this friend. We all miss that bird.

Work Problems

Another job I did after my stitches came out was to scrape the walks between the barns. I slipped on the ice one day and hurt my back, landing so hard, I was sent back to see the nurse immediately. Each time I was sent to the nurse, it seemed I got more work just out of spite. I went back to working as if nothing ever happened, trying not to show that I was almost constantly in pain. I didn't tell my mom how bad I was hurting for a long time either.

I knew Mom would feel bad, and I was an adult and responsible for myself. Even though this job was really too hard for me, I hadn't been able to find another one. I can't type or do computer work well enough to get an office job because my hands have so many tumors and are also somewhat twisted. I had applied for every job I thought I might be able to handle.

By now I was walking very erratically, my hands hurt constantly, my back hurt most of the time, and I had lots of headaches.

One part of the work I did every day was scraping the rooms. There were forty-eight crates in each room. The back gate of the crate was opened, and a long-handled scraper was used to remove the waste. Feeding the room was done first. Each feeder, if it was dirty, had to be dumped and cleaned before fresh feed was given. I started timing myself to see how long it took to feed each room and then how long it took to scrape. I thought my timing was good, as long as the gates and feeders did not have problems. My time was thirty minutes if all went well.

The farm manager was not a people person, and he thought he was so good. One day he told me I needed to speed up my work, so I told him if he could do a room faster than my time, I would work on shaving time off my work. He refused to even see if he could do better. I'm willing to bet he could not do much better, if any at all.

Work never did get any better. I was up for my evaluation, and they had the manager from another farm do mine because my manager could not speak enough English. I was told that I was not doing well because of the language barrier and that since I did not speak or understand Spanish and the other workers did not speak English, "It would help if you learned Spanish."

I asked why I should learn Spanish when this is the USA.

He said, "That can be taken as a discriminatory remark."

My answer was that my being asked to learn Spanish could be taken as a discriminatory remark too, because when I'm working and someone doesn't understand my words, then we use gestures. It seemed to me they were the ones with the problems, and why should it be held against me?

All of the safety meetings were done in Spanish. I had taken a conversational Spanish class through Seward County Community College, but it wasn't enough to allow me to converse with Hispanic people who talked so fast and mostly ignored me. I knew this was against company policy, as my presence was required at the meetings, and I didn't understand anything that was said; no interpreter was there. By now, I knew they were just looking for any reason to let me go, but I would not give them the satisfaction of quitting. I did file a complaint about being required to attend the safety meetings and not having an interpreter there so I could know what they talked about.

During the time after breaking my leg, I had bought a three-bedroom mobile home. Mom and Darrel let me put it on their property in the country, about one hundred yards from their house. They helped me get it all set up and move into it. Soon after that, I had more surgery in Garden City to remove the rod from my leg. I thought that after the rod was removed I would be able to walk much better and this would be the end of my work problems, but it was far from it.

Cancer Diagnosis

My neurologist, Dr. Schaeffer, decided I needed to see another doctor in Lubbock,

Texas. So Mom and Darrel took me there, along with the latest MRI I had. Dr. Smith looked at the MRI and told us, "Do you see all these black specks? That is cancer."

Mom immediately began to cry, and Dr. Smith said there wasn't anything he could do for me, so we told Darrel to get us out of there!

I returned to work, putting up with a lot of garbage from the staff at the farm. I was still processing and power washing, since my hand had healed from the carpal tunnel surgery. It was still uncomfortable, but I tolerated it.

Soon I had more surgery, this time to remove some of the larger tumors that were causing me pain and getting in the way. Some on my breasts were larger in volume than the breasts themselves, and they were painful. I wasn't at all happy with the surgeon who did this; she didn't wait for the anesthetic to take effect before she started cutting on me, stating she was in a hurry, then she didn't even take time to talk to my dad, who had driven me to Amarillo for the procedure.

The same day as that surgery, I also had a full spine MRI. This showed that I had tumors inside my spinal column, which was not good news at all. Once again, I returned to work as if nothing had happened. But my problems continued. My back began to hurt a lot, and I started weaving when I walked. This was caught by the breeding team leader, who sent me to the company nurse. She said I had seventy-two hours to see a neurologist, and I had to be off those three days with no pay and call in every day. Then she sent me to my primary doctor, who got me in to see a neurologist, but the soonest he could get me an appointment was in three months.

Seaboard had to allow me to work until then, since the appointment was made within the seventy-two hours. Neurologists are specialists, and it is common for them to be booked up months in advance.

Mom and Darrel took me to Amarillo to see Dr. Cone, and his finding was that I needed a stenosis release. This involved nibbling out some of the bone in that area of the spine, as the bone had overgrown and was crowding the cord. Mom and Darrel were always faithful to take me to the doctors, and Mom always stayed with me when I was in the hospital. This time, we had a cloth with Scripture verses on healing, and after gaining permission to do so, she tied it around my ankle before they took me into surgery. Dr. Cone and I both expected me to be able to return to work in six weeks. After that time had passed and I was still in pain and having to walk with a walker again, I was given a year from when my leave started to return to work.

My doctor never released me, so exactly one year from when I went on leave; I received a letter of termination by certified mail. I was rather relieved, because several times, my manager did not believe I had anything wrong with me; he thought that I was faking it so I could get out of working and get others to do my work. I really was not able to work anyway.

The Next Step—Disability

Now I had to apply for disability, which was not a simple task. I had to prove that I really could no longer work. Those in the disability office kept questioning why I couldn't go back to one of my former jobs, like the bus aid job. How was I going to be able to help handicapped kids up onto the bus when I wasn't able to climb on myself? I was denied disability the first time, and I reapplied.

Getting Social Security disability is not a simple matter, or at least it wasn't for me. Finally, after three long years and being denied three times, my mom's good friend, Carol Ann Sewell, told her that she had a friend who worked for Social Security. She went and talked to her, and was told, "Yes, I know about Beth, but I don't think we are going to be able to help her."

Carol Ann asked why, and she said because I was so young. Then Carol Ann told her, "But if you could only *see* this girl!"

When my friend told me this, I took several photos of Beth, showing how disabled she was, and got statements from some of her doctors saying she was disabled and why, and mailed those to the SS office. Because of this dear friend's help, Beth was awarded her disability, retroactive back to the time of the back surgery. Praise God for friends!

After Beth had received word she was approved for Social Security disability, I called the lady at SS who had helped us and asked if we could come to Dodge City and meet her and possibly take her to lunch. She said she would be happy to meet us for lunch but could in no way allow us to pay for hers, as that is forbidden by SS rules. We met her and enjoyed lunch with her; and she could see that Beth really was in need. She was barely walking on a walker at that time.

I had sent her a card and a note of thanks for her help, and she told us I was the only client who had ever bothered to say thank you to her for helping them in all her years of working for the Social Security Administration.

Because Dr. Smith had said Beth had cancer in her spine, I decided to have a surprise party for her forty-second birthday, August 28, 2004. She could barely walk now, even with a walker, and was losing the use of her right hand. Never had I imagined, even with the progression of the NF, that my sweet daughter would be disabled before her forty-second birthday! It seemed so cruel, so unbelievable! Because of the cancer diagnosis, we didn't know how much longer she would be with us.

I arranged to have a friend of hers bring her into the church fellowship hall in her wheelchair. Many friends and family came to wish her well. Our friend, Kay Grice, made two beautiful birthday cakes, and we served a complete supper. Beth's dad was there that night too. I remember introducing all the family who were present to her guests.

So many people sent cards, flowers and gifts, and many came to wish her well. It was a special celebration for a special girl.

It turned out the diagnosis of spinal cancer was wrong, for which we thank God. Another doctor told us those black specks were probably just something on the film. It seemed that Beth's entire life was falling apart, but still she kept her head up, maintained her faith in God, looked to the future, and believed things would get better.

My Prince Charming
—Beth—

I bought my mom's computer when she upgraded to a newer model. I found an NF chat room that I started visiting, and I started talking to others who also had NF. We talked about the various ways our NF affects us. It was in that chat room that I made friends with several people, and among them was a man named John Hamelin. He and I began to chat on the computer and learn about each other's lives.

In September of 2002, I flew to Dallas because I wanted to go to a family camp just for NF patients and their families in Burton, Texas. At the camp, I met at least six people I had talked to online. Becki Radick and I became close friends, since we are close in age and had a lot in common. On our way back to Dallas after the camp was over, instead of talking, Becki and I wrote notes back and forth to keep things quiet. I told her about John and that he was to call me when I got home.

John did call, and for a few weeks he called every Friday. I got a prepaid calling card, which is what he was using to call me. Then we took turns calling each other every Friday at 6:00 p.m. In June of 2003, John flew from New York to come to Kansas and see me. He even wanted to attend my family reunion! (Mom said he was a brave man!) He rode the train and got to Garden City early in the morning. I was still able to drive then, and I went to pick him up. My friend Mindi lives not far from Garden City, and she wanted to meet John and also do the driving so I could show him around without having to drive.

He arrived around 7:00 in the morning, and I knew it was him by the Yankees shirt he was wearing. John has NF too, but his is a much milder case than mine. He didn't even know he had it until he tried to enlist in the army when he was eighteen years old. They turned him down because of it. He was really shocked, as he had never heard of it before then.

John is very small and thin, with black hair, dark eyes, and very thick black eyebrows. If you didn't know anything about NF, you would never suspect that he had it, but Mom and I both recognized it immediately. There is a certain look that we have that gives it away, even without seeing the tumors. John has only a very few tumors on his face, maybe three, but has many tiny ones in a band on either side of his spine. He is still able to live alone, work, drive, and live a normal life. So that is a real blessing.

His dad never knew John had NF, as John never told him before his dad died. John went to the reunion with us, which was held that year at my aunt Shirley Williams's house near Admire, Kansas. Mom and Darrel took their pickup, pulling the fifth-wheel trailer, and John and I followed in my car.

At my family reunion, John met a lot of my family. My aunt Doris Miller even got him to participate in the talent show! He, being a city boy, did not have the foggiest notion what he was doing being part of a skit where the words did not make a lot of sense to his big city ears. There was something about shooting a bar, instead of a bear, and he didn't get it at first, but he was a good sport. Everyone who met him liked him and made him feel right at home.

This time seems almost like a fairy tale to me: I thought I would never have a boyfriend, much less one who would come so far to see me, accept me and all my family, and just be comfortable with all of us. My whole extended family was really happy for me too and expressed appreciation to John for coming.

John and I made several detours and stops on the way back home so he could see some of what Kansas has to offer. We went to the Cosmosphere in Hutchinson; to Greensburg to see the world's largest hand-dug well; and we stopped in Dodge City to see the Boot Hill Museum on Front Street and have an old-time photo taken. I was a saloon girl, and he was a mean cowboy with a rifle. At this time I was walking with a cane.

Later in the week, we went to Liberal to visit Dorothy's house from the *Wizard of Oz*. We also visited the Liberal Air Museum. Then we went on to Boise City, Oklahoma, so he could meet my dad, two aunts, and a cousin. We went to the museum there and had our picture taken standing by the life-sized steel dinosaur.

When it came time for John to leave, I drove him to Garden to catch his train. As he was leaving, I imagined myself running alongside the train like a woman I saw once in the movies when her man was leaving. John had finally gotten the courage to tell me he loved me, and I was in seventh heaven! I never expected to find a man who would see me in such a condition and still find me lovable. God is so good! Every day I thank and praise Him for John and what a difference he makes in my life.

John continued to contact Beth often via computer as long as she was able to use her computer. He also called often, and this contact with him kept Beth's spirits up in a wonderful way, adding a refreshing new dimension to her life.

Beth and John have many friends from the NF chat room, all of who have a different story of how NF affects their lives. During the nearly ten years they have been chatting with them, at least ten of their friends have lost their lives, most of them because of NF-related cancers.

They worked out a schedule for John's calls so she would know when to expect them and he would know the times she would be out of her room for Bingo, Penny Ante, or other activities. She tells all the nurses and CNAs about John, and they are all so happy that Beth has found the man who truly loves her.

John does love Beth with a deep and abiding love. He has never seemed the least bit put off by any of her disabilities, even as they continue to worsen. What a blessing he is in her life! A friend remarked just days ago that John doesn't treat Beth as if she has any disability at all but rather as if she has nothing wrong!

John continues to shower Beth with cards, flowers, tee shirts, and other gifts—anything he finds that he thinks will make her smile. She has quite a collection of stuffed bears for Valentine's and other holidays, all from him. He has also become very romantic in his notes and calls to her, which she loves.

HOW CAN WE HELP?

I n October of 2003, Beth talked it over with John and then asked me what I thought about her going to Dodge City for a while to rehab. She had a doctor over there, and he agreed to put her in rehab and see if we could regain some of her mobility. She stayed there for two weeks, and it did help some, for a short time. She was still walking, but with difficulty.

Through the years, we have tried many things in the hope of helping Beth. Some things helped for a time; many others were only money thrown away. We have a garage full of gadgets designed to help a handicapped person, such as dressing sticks, overhead rails with grab bars for her bed, a hospital bed, canes, a walker, toilet riser, two wheelchairs, and a power chair. This is visible proof that hope is always with us, beckoning us forward. The last big purchase, for which Beth begged, was a NuStep exercise machine. She may have been able to get on it twice, and it was very expensive. Now it sits in the garage too.

Of course, we had high hopes that going to rehab would benefit Beth, but it was another in a long string of disappointments.

As the NF relentlessly eroded her strength, Beth's walking became erratic. She had many NF friends she had met in their chat room, and one of them, Joe, and his wife, Diane, came from Illinois to meet her in person. I drove Beth to Dodge City to meet them at Boot Hill. After we had visited a bit and taken photos, we went to the Golden Corral to eat. Beth was using a walker by this time, so I went to the buffet with her, carried her plate, and got her food for her. As we were going back to the table, Beth said, "I'm stuck."

"What do you mean?" I asked.

She said, "My feet won't move."

I took her plate and set it on the table; then I went back to her and had to physically move first one foot, then the other for her, all the way to the table. As a mom, this was heartrending for me. I could barely choke back the tears and try to visit with her friends, wondering what was next for this lovely young woman. Hadn't she suffered enough? Why was this happening to her?

A few days later, as she was coming down the three steps from her trailer, her feet "got stuck" again, and again, I had to move them for her. These experiences brought me to the painful realization that she may not be able to walk at all much longer.

Beth's dad heard about a clinic in Midland, Texas, that he was convinced could help Beth. A friend of his had told him about it and spoke of it in glowing terms. He asked Darrel and me to take Beth there, saying he would cover all the expenses she incurred during her stay. So we made the long drive to Midland, with hope riding in the car with us—an almost tangible thing!

This clinic was strange, to say the least. When I asked what specialty the doctor there was in, I was told they had no doctor, but they did have a nurse—on call! I have no idea what training the personnel there had, but some of the things they were doing were very unorthodox.

They had people sitting around a big room with IVs running in their arms, and we were told they were giving them Vitamin C through those. Other things done there were several kinds of cosmetic surgery, such as eyeliner and lip liner being tattooed on, partial face lifts and eye lifts.

I visited with several of the "patients" there and learned they were being treated for cancer, diabetes, heart disease, various skin problems, and vitamin/mineral deficiencies. That made me wonder at the validity of this clinic, especially when there was neither a doctor nor a nurse in attendance. But we had promised her dad we would give it a try, so we went ahead and put Beth in treatment.

They gave Beth the IVs of Vitamin C; also Vitamin C in a powdered form to mix with water and drink; put her under different colors of light, blue, especially; rubbed various creams and ointments on her; sprayed her skin with something that dried shiny and stiff, gave her various kinds of enemas, and took photos of her every day. We were there for three days while they did all this stuff, staying in a motel at night.

Each morning, they would show us the pictures, comparing them to the ones from the day before and saying, "Look! See how the tumors are shrinking? See how much smoother her skin is already?" But we could see no difference, in spite of all their enthusiasm and efforts to convince us.

Beth was barely walking at this time. They were doing construction on the street in front of the clinic, and the parking lot was across that street. When we came to pick her up one day, she managed to walk, holding on to me, out to the middle of the street, where she got stuck. I wasn't able to help her and didn't know what to do! One of the workmen saw that we were in distress and came and helped me get her to the other side of the street where the car was, and how we appreciated his help!

They sent her home with bags full of pills and powders, and she took them for a while, but when she didn't feel better, function better, or look better, she decided it was all quackery and threw away the rest. This was another in the long list of things we did in an effort to get help for Beth, only to be disappointed again.

—Beth—

Another Family Reunion

In June 2005, John came to Kansas again, this time for our reunion in Hershey, Nebraska, at my aunt Doris and uncle Vernon Miller's place. This time, he flew, and we drove to Dodge City to pick him up. I could barely walk with a walker by now, and so Mom borrowed a wheelchair to use at the reunion. We went back to Boot Hill and had another photo taken. In this one, we were dressed in old-time clothes and behind us was a sign saying, "Get the heck out of Dodge!"

We had a good time at this reunion too, even though it was so cold, we all had to wear coats, and they used a wood-burning stove in the garage where we were meeting to keep us warm.

Hershey is not far from North Platte, Nebraska, and they were having a big Nebraska land rodeo there. Neither John nor I had ever been to a rodeo, so he really enjoyed that. I was still walking a little bit then, and it took every ounce of my willpower and every ounce of Mom's and John's strength to get me up those bleacher steps to row 17! We were still bundled up in winter coats, and it was mid-June. It's still a joke in the family about the year we had to wear our coats in June. When the rodeo was over, I could not get back down the steps, so my cousin's husband carried me down on his back. That was the last year my dad was able to come to the reunion. All of the family still liked him, even Mom, and he was always welcome.

I decided to accept John's invitation to go back to New York with him. His mom was still living, and I would stay with them there. Since we hadn't booked the trip together, we didn't get to sit together on the plane. I could barely walk but was given a seat in the very back of the plane, and John was seated nearer to the front. I had to have help to get to my assigned seat. One person across the aisle from me asked to move to an empty seat closer to the front, leaving that seat empty. I asked the flight attendant if John could sit there; she went to tell him, but the guy in the middle seat moved to the aisle seat before she came back. He was not asked to move, so John could not sit there. I always thought it uncaring of that man.

I took my own wheelchair on that trip, so John was able to take me several places during the remaining week of his vacation. We went to the Syracuse Zoo, where we saw penguins, Asian elephants, tigers, lions, and bears, oh my!

I visited John at his home four times, twice at Christmas and twice in the summer. I got to meet all of his family and some of his friends, and he took me lots of places, including the New York State Fair.

John came back to see me for Christmas in 2004. We had Christmas at my mom's house, and my dad, his sister, my sisters, my brother and his daughter, were all there that year. We were all there except my sister Kerri, and she was missed dearly.

I could still walk a little bit, and John and I danced one dance to an Elvis Presley Christmas song. It's the only dance we ever shared, but it brought us closer together as a couple. John got to experience a Kansas winter, but that year there was not much snow, certainly not like what he gets in New York.

Back to Surgery

After John went home, I was on my computer on Sunday, January 23, 2005, instant messaging with him, when my brother Jim called me to tell me my dad had died in his sleep. This saddened me beyond words because my dad and I were getting closer as time went by. A couple weeks before this, Mom had taken me to our primary doctor in Ulysses, Dr. Geoffrey Plumlee. He checked me over and told me I needed to have more surgery—this time on my neck.

I said, "I don't want to have more surgery! If I don't have it, what will happen?"

He answered, "If you don't have it, Beth, you will die."

A recent MRI had shown a small tumor growing in my neck, and my doctors felt it was life threatening and needed to be removed as soon as possible. With a big sigh, I answered, "Well, I guess I'll have it, then."

This tumor was pressing the area of my spinal cord that controls breathing, and so my choice was to have surgery or die. The appointment was made, again with Dr. Cone in Amarillo. But first I had to get through my dad's funeral.

Mom, Diane, and I went to Boise City on Monday, January 24, to pick out the casket and flowers, write the obituary, and make whatever other arrangements needed to be made. We chose a blue casket and his blue suit for him to wear. These choices were not easy and took a while. Diane and I were the two children who were available to make these decisions, since the others lived too far away or had not taken the day off work to go.

My four nephews and a cousin's son were the pallbearers, and all were Boy Scouts. Three of them were Eagle Scouts, and he was carried out with honors. My two nieces, Katy and Abby, were flower girls, walking behind the casket, carrying bouquets of flowers.

As soon as possible, after the nice dinner the church provided for the family, we said our good-byes, and Mom, Diane, and I headed for Amarillo for my surgery.

When my sister Kerri, who didn't want to seem too mushy, said good-bye to me, she said, "Bye, Beth—don't croak!"

When we got to Amarillo, I had to be checked into the hospital, and Mom and Diane prayed with me. I could feel they were afraid for me, but I honestly didn't have any fear, as I knew God wasn't finished with me yet. I am not sure what His purpose is for keeping me on this earth, but if I survived the car wreck, He must have something He wants me to do yet.

Just before I was wheeled away to surgery the next morning, Mom was trying to keep a cheerful face and when they came to wheel me to surgery she kissed me and said the same thing Kerri had said to me in a joking way.

I asked, "How will I know if I die?"

My sister Diane quickly answered, "You will see Jesus!"

Dr. Cone was upfront with us about how very serious this surgery was. He said he couldn't guarantee Beth would live through it, not only because he would be working right against the fragile spinal cord, but also because it would require her lying face down for the surgery, dangerous for the length of time it would require, especially considering her breathing difficulty.

Diane and I were very concerned and prayed for Beth during the surgery. Some friends from Amarillo came and sat with us for a time, but our minds were so consumed with Beth and our prayers for her that we barely heard what they were saying. After two hours, Dr. Cone came into the room, and we jumped up and went to talk to him.

He assured us she had come through the surgery just fine. He told us that he had expected the tumor to be the size of a pencil eraser, but when he got in there, the thing was as big as his thumb! Now that doesn't sound very big, he said, until you realize that the space it was occupying was normally the size of a pencil lead! While it was microscopic surgery, it certainly was not a microscopic tumor. He had to take out a quarter inch of a vertebra to get to it, and he had to cut the tumor into four pieces to get it out.

He said, "No wonder she was having trouble breathing!" But, he said, the good news was that it was only attached and being fed by a few very small threads of tissue and that he got it all and did not think it would grow back. God had come through for us again!

The Scriptures show us so very clearly that nothing in life is wasted if we love and serve God. No matter how sharp the bend in the road, no matter how disruptive the crisis, everything that happens to us is for the eternal purposes of God. He is training us through the process. Like any worthy parent, He wants to teach us what we cannot learn any other way. With each crisis in her life, both Beth and I were forced to depend more and more on God.

We know He loves us, we know He wants the very best for us, and we have to trust Him with everything, especially the painful times when we see clearly that He is all we have. And when He is all we have, we learn that He is all we need. "The Lord is my light and my salvation—whom shall I fear? The Lord is the strength of my life—of whom shall I be afraid?" (Psalm 27:1, KJV).

John sent Beth a lovely bouquet of flowers and a big teddy bear. This was the first of many times for him to do that. And each time, she asked me to take pictures of her with them.

Diane stayed until Beth was out of danger. Jim and his daughter Katy came to see Beth, and she appreciated her siblings for caring.

—Beth—

I'm Getting Tired of Hospitals

The last time I was visiting John in New York, in 2005, I had planned to stay a longer time, but John was working, and his house has some stairs inside that I couldn't manage; also I couldn't get up from the couch if I sat there, so I had to spend the entire day in my wheelchair until he came home. This caused pain and swelling in my legs. The bed I slept in was high, and I fell off the bed and couldn't get up. His sister and brother-in-law had to come and help me up. I called Mom and told her how hard it was for me, and she advised me to call and change my ticket and come back home. So that is what I did.

I arrived home from New York on a Saturday in January of 2006. I was still living in my mobile home. Darrel and Mom had made modifications to it to make it easier for me, such as adding a ramp, widening the doors, taking up the carpet and putting down linoleum to make it easier to move my chair, and replacing the bathtub with a shower with grab bars for safety.

On Sunday evening, I was hungry for some spaghetti and thought I could cook that for myself. I had it all planned. I filled a big pot with water, put it on the stove, got it to boiling, and cooked the spaghetti. I folded a heavy bath towel and put it in my lap in the wheelchair. Then I set the pot of boiling water on the towel, because I needed both hands to move the wheelchair. The idea was to roll myself over to the sink so I could drain the water off the spaghetti. But … the pan upset, and the boiling mess went right down both my knees and legs.

I called Mom, but she was at church. Darrel came over, got my sweatpants and my socks off me, and called 911. Then he called Mom at church to tell her what had happened. It took a while for them to come with the ambulance, and then they took their time putting an IV in my arm before taking me to the emergency room. Mom was waiting there for me. The doctor on call looked me over, put some Silvadene cream on my legs, and said I could go home!

Mom came to my rescue again, saying no, she didn't think I should go home while in so much pain and that she wanted Dr. Plumlee to see me before I was dismissed. So they admitted me to the hospital and gave me something for the pain. There were huge blisters on my legs, and the pain was really bad.

When Dr. Plumlee came in the next morning, he couldn't believe the other doctor had wanted to send me home. He said, "She will be here for a while."

And sure enough, I was in the hospital for a whole month while they treated the burns. Everything had to be sterile; bandages had to be changed very carefully each day, and my pain needed to be controlled. Why the on-call doctor had wanted to send me home is more than I can understand.

My mom said, "Honey, the next time you get hungry for spaghetti, call Mom!"

After I went home, the home health nurse came every other day for about two months to wash the wounds and change the dressings. I really appreciated them taking care of me. During this time, Mom's friend, Pat Ethridge, came once a week to clean the house for me. She knew I wasn't able to do it, and her help was so much appreciated. She became a special friend to me, too.

While I was recovering from the burns, Dr. Plumlee ordered a power chair for me. This made my life a lot easier, as I could drive it up and down the ramp to my house and into and out of the handicapped equipped van we had bought. My mobile home really didn't have enough room to maneuver the power chair around well, so I still used the wheel chair when at home.

Sliding Further Downhill

It took a long time for my legs to heal, partly because the skin on my left shin was thin, as I'd had a huge neurofibroma removed from that area. Also, I was steadily losing strength and mobility. I kept trying to do things but really couldn't manage to do very much. And more and more neurofibromas appeared all over my body, including my face and neck. My hands were looking really bad by now too.

Mom asked me if I would consider moving over to her house. She teaches painting classes and has a nice room she uses for her studio. It has its own bathroom, and that would have made it so much easier for her to help me, bring me meals, etc. But I said no.

LETTERS FROM BETH

I n 2006, Both Darrel and I attended a Walk to Emmaus. Part of that is your sponsors get special people in your life to write you letters, expressing what you mean in their lives. Darrel attended the first one, and I went two weeks later. These letters were written for that occasion.

Beth has always expressed herself well in writing. I would like to copy here a letter to Darrel which she wrote when she was barely able to write anymore. Her handwriting is quite shaky, she could barely hold a pen, but it is still legible.

> Dear Darrel,
> When you married Mom, I really didn't know what to think of you. You didn't

know what to think of me either! I was just thankful you were sent to be with Mom.

We've had a lot of ups and downs since then. I'm proud to have you as a Dad; you've gone beyond duty as a step-dad. Since my disability has gone from bad to worse, you've not thrown in the towel, but have stayed encouraging to both Mom and me.

You outdid yourself in January, when I spilled the boiling water on myself. You came and helped me get socks and pants off, and put ice on the burns. You called 911 and got Mom notified. Then you stayed with me until I left.

Thank you for all you've done and do.

I love you,
Beth

And a couple of weeks later, she wrote the following letter to me:

Dear Mom,

Thank you for being my Mom. Knowing I was a little different from siblings after age 4, but you never treated me differently or made a big deal about it.

In 1997, when I was in that car wreck, you put your life on hold so you could help get me through a close tragedy. All those days I was in ICU, you hung onto God's out-stretched hand and to His Word. You sang to me, cried with me and held me in your arms. You never let me give in to the pain, and told me, "Show Satan that what he intended for evil, God will use for good."

Now, my disability has reared its ugly head, and you've been more than encouraging and supportive. In January, when I burned myself, I could see the concern in your face.

Thank you for all you've done, and all that is yet to come.

I love you,
Beth

When Beth became unable to get into and out of our car, we purchased a handicapped-equipped van with a sliding ramp she could drive her power chair up and down so we could still take her places. It was hard for me to take her places by myself because of the problem of getting her to the bathroom and handling her there. But the van served us well for a couple of years; we were able to take her to doctor appointments, to church, and to the family reunion. She had to have a catheter and leg bag in order for us to take her on trips overnight or longer. And there were enough others there at the reunion to help me with her at other times.

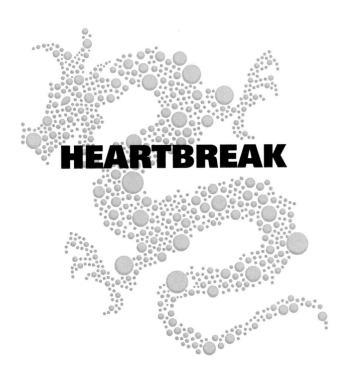

HEARTBREAK

By this time, Beth was forty-three years old and experiencing frequent falls and was unable to get up. She would manage to scoot on her rear to the phone and call me. If Darrel was home, he and I would go over and get her up. It was good that she lived on our property, close enough for us to keep an eye on her and help her. One day she fell while trying to get out of bed; Darrel was gone, and I picked her up and put her back on the bed by myself. That took every ounce of my strength, and if God hadn't helped me, I couldn't have done it, because Beth is four inches taller and probably thirty pounds heavier than I am.

I offered to drop my classes and turn the studio into an apartment for her, but she wouldn't hear of it. I asked, "Why not?"

And her answer was that she had promised years ago that she would take care of me when I got old, and she didn't want me to have to take care of her! I told her I appreciated that offer and knew she meant it and would if she could, but her circumstances were different now. Still, she refused.

It got to the point that she was calling me several times a day to come over and help her. Sometimes she could get to the toilet, but she couldn't get up. (We had a riser and rails for her.) Or she would try to transfer from her wheelchair to the bed or another chair, and fall. By this time, she had a power wheelchair, but still she had problems.

One morning she called me to come help her seven times before noon! I was so distressed and frustrated, and I didn't know what to do. That was the one time I truly understood why a man will sometimes punch his fist through a wall!

The next day, I went to Dr. Plumlee's office and asked him, "Could you give me an anti-depressant or something?"

He could tell I was close to tears, so he asked, "What's going on?"

I explained to him, and he said he didn't think I was depressed; he just thought I was overloaded.

He took me by the shoulders, looked me in the eyes, and said, "You can't *do* this anymore! Do you hear me? You're through! You're going to mess up your back, and then you won't be any good to Beth, to Darrel, or to yourself! You've got to face the fact that Beth has to go to the care home." Then he made an appointment for Dr.

Cone and Beth's other doctors in Amarillo to check her over again.

Early in May 2006, we took Beth to Baptist St. Anthony Hospital in Amarillo, where she was tested, and they ran MRIs and such for three days. Their findings were that she had neurofibromas growing inside her spinal column all the way from her tailbone to the base of her skull; there was also one in her brain pond.

Dr. Cone said he was in hopes they would find one or two big ones that were responsible for her downhill slide that he could remove; but he couldn't remove all of them! Her endocrinologist, Dr. Steven Usala, said that Beth's problems were increasing, but there wasn't really any treatment available. Both of these are wonderful, kind, and caring physicians; they had gone more than the second mile trying to help Beth.

When they told her, "It's time to think about placement," Beth went ballistic! She yelled and cried, telling them to let her go home and at least *try* to take care of herself, and she said she would kill herself before she would go to the nursing home. I didn't believe she would really do that, and she told me later she wouldn't have, but the doctors believed her. So they said they would only release her if she would be taken to the Ulysses hospital and then transitioned from there to the care home.

We had picked up a copy of the *Amarillo!* magazine, which contained photos of an outdoor exhibit of the Stations of the Cross in Groom, Texas. Beth really wanted to go see it, and since it wasn't all that far out of our way, we drove over there.

We could see a huge cross for miles before we got to the location. There, we saw numerous cast figures of Jesus during the last days before the crucifixion, and then carrying and falling under the cross, being crucified... and then the empty tomb, testifying to His resurrection. It is a beautifully done tribute to the One who died for us, and we took lots of pictures there. I was happy we were able to fulfill this wish for Beth. When we got back to Ulysses, we took Beth to the hospital, where we left her crying. I was crying too.

In the next few days, the assistant director of nursing at the care home came to evaluate Beth. At first, the director of the home, Billie Upshaw, said she didn't think they could accept her because of her young age; she was concerned they couldn't meet her social needs. I explained that Beth didn't really have a social life because of her degree of disability. They assured Beth she could have her computer in her room so she could maintain contact with her NF friends, but, sadly, they would not let her have her little Mieka dog there, even though she was well trained.

Dr. Plumlee used all the influence he could bring to bear to get them to let her have her dog there, but nothing swayed them. This was another heartbreak for Beth. So Mieka had to come live with Darrel and me, and I brought her to visit Beth often. Beth was admitted to Western Prairie Care Home, the same one where she had worked as a CNA her last two years of high school. It was May 23, 2006, and she was forty-three years old.

What a horrible day that was, for her and for me; it was absolutely heartbreaking. I have told people that I know it is hard to have to enter a parent into a nursing home; my dad was there for eight years before his death, and my mom was there at that time, so I know. But if you multiply that by about a thousand, you would have an idea how it feels to have to put your *child* there.

A few days after she entered the home, I drove Beth to the library. She has always loved books and reading. On the way there, she said in a tear-choked voice, "Mom, why didn't you fight for me?"

I answered, in tears, "Beth, you have no idea how long or how hard I have fought for you! And if you're going to make me cry every time I see you, I don't know how we are going to get through this!"

Beth was mad at the entire world, and especially at me, because she blamed me for her having to go into the home, for about six months. She thought the decision had been mine when; really, the doctors had made the decision. She kept saying, "I don't belong here with all these *old* people!"

I tried to encourage her to get to know the people there and that everyone needs friends; she could be a shining light there in the darkness. But she was so hurt and so angry at God, and at me, that she went into a depression for several months.

I kept telling Beth that as soon as she was able to get into and out of bed by herself and take care of herself in the bathroom, she could go back home. Sadly, this never happened.

Gloria is also a resident of the home, and is the person nearest in age to Beth. They became friends and began spending time together, going out into the courtyard in the fresh air and sunshine, visiting and watching the pet rabbit and the turtles that lived out there.

But after some months had passed, I noticed they were visiting less and less, so I asked Beth about it. She told me that Gloria was always so negative, and that when she tried to lift her up, Gloria got worse and ended up dragging Beth down, so she felt that for her own good, she needed to spend less time with her. They are still friends, and Gloria is still negative. Everyone tries to get her to be more positive, but she resists with all her might!

In 2007, Laura, the bookkeeper at the home who had become friends with Beth, encouraged her to write about her life using her computer. Beth had some use of both hands at that time, and she typed out twenty-seven pages. I cannot imagine the hours that took her, as her coordination has never been really good, and she never took a typing or keyboarding class. It is from those pages that I am taking the quotes used in this book. She is able to express herself really well in writing and did a tremendous job.

I'm so glad she wrote her own story then, because by 2008 she had completely lost the use of her right hand. Beth gradually adjusted to her new reality, and her normal good humor returned. After about a year, I said to her, "Beth, what's going on? You used to be so grouchy, and now you are getting sweeter and sweeter!"

Her answer was, "Well, Mom, I just decided that if this is the way it has to be, I might as well make the best of it. I don't think God would be pleased by me being down and grouchy all the time."

And she grows still sweeter all the time. What a blessing!

After Beth began losing the use of her right hand, it wasn't long until she could no longer hold a book and turn the pages, so she had to give up reading, heartbreak on heartbreak. Holly Mathes, her friend since high school, who is now our librarian, ordered her a tape player and gave us a big catalog of books on tape. Beth did listen to some of them, but she wasn't able to turn the machine on and off and switch the tapes by herself, and help wasn't always available. We bought her a Sony Reader, but she wasn't able to use that either.

At first, they used a sit-to-stand lift to help Beth move from bed to chair, etc. When they had to switch to the sling lift, she resisted with all her might, as she did every change that signaled further deterioration of her abilities. It was so painful to watch and to hear.

Another change soon after this was that her body could no longer signal her need to urinate. For a while, the nurses catheterized her several times a day, but eventually the doctor ordered an indwelling catheter for her. This made it easier on both her and her caregivers, but was disheartening because it was another degree of disability for her. Eventually, they also gave up on taking her to the bathroom for her stools, and she had to suffer the indignity of wearing Attends.

She began to watch TV more and more, as that was about all she could do. But her choices were wholesome ones: Christian programs and game shows, mostly, along with movies about animals, and comedies. She also had a DVR and could record some shows to watch later. Her caregivers were really sweet about doing that for her, as well as lots of other little things.

During this time, she wasn't hearing from John much, and that bothered her a lot. When she did hear, he was grouchy and snappy. John said he hadn't been to a doctor in thirty years. And one day, when his brother was visiting him, John passed out, and they took him to the hospital and found his blood sugar was 1400! His doctor said he didn't know how he survived that.

They got it down, taught John what to eat and how to take his meds and manage his diabetes, which, of course, was the problem. He took excellent care of himself and eventually was able to get off insulin and take only pills. And he became his own sweet self again, much to Beth's joy. We hadn't known anything about this scary episode until he was much better.

SHADOW OF DEATH

In 2007, I was advised to take Beth to the hospital for a sonogram on her stomach, and we were told she had gallstones. They weren't bothering her at that time, though, so nothing was done.

Two years later, Darrel and I were gone on a trip to Thailand and Viet Nam, and when we got home, Beth said Dr. B. had told her she needed immediate surgery for the gallstones. She refused to have it until I got home, so when we did; as soon as the arrangements could be made she went to the hospital, where Dr. B. removed her gallbladder using a laparoscope through her navel. She stayed in the hospital overnight and then was taken back to the care home. A new facility had been built, and all the residents moved into it a few weeks prior to this incident.

About the third day post-surgery, Beth began feeling sick. She told the nurses, and they called the doctor; he did not come. She got progressively sicker. Dr. B. was called again, and after two weeks, he finally came. He stood by her recliner, looked at her, and told her that he always tells his gallbladder surgery patients that it takes two weeks to recover. And, he said, since she wasn't ambulatory, she should give it another two weeks … and he left. He didn't check her, do any kind of tests at all, ask if she was eating, nothing.

Beth got sicker and sicker; she couldn't eat anything at all, and the nurses were very concerned for her. I was working at the home, cooking, on another hall, and the nurse from her hall—sweet, caring, and wonderful Sondra Patton—came to tell me she was worse. Of course, I went to her room immediately and could see for myself that she was very sick.

I asked them to call Dr. B.; again, they did, and he didn't come. The nurses kept calling and faxing Dr. B. and asking him to come; he kept putting them off with things like, "I'm really busy, maybe this afternoon," or "Maybe I can make it tomorrow." (It is only a few blocks from the home to the hospital!)

Finally, into the *fifth* week after surgery, Rita Gutierrez—another wonderful, caring nurse—called Dr. Plumlee and said, "Dr. Plumlee, Beth is sick. She's *really* sick! She needs a doctor! Get your butt up here *now!*"

Dr. Plumlee came immediately, took one look at Beth and at the contents of her catheter bag, which were darker than coffee, and called the ambulance. Back she went to the Ulysses hospital, and once again, Dr. B. performed surgery on her—this time to install two JP drains, because he said she had a bile leak. He was going to keep her there, but Dr. Plumlee said no way. "She is too sick for us to keep her here; she needs to go to a bigger hospital where they have more specialists and better equipment."

Dr. B. spoke to me after the gallstone surgery and said, "I think you already know that the NF is going to take Beth's life at an early age. Parents never feel their children should die before them. But you don't have anything to feel guilty about; you've done everything perfectly." (I haven't; I'm human!)

"Those neurofibromas are growing on every organ in her body," he continued, "and have multiplied just since I did that last surgery. And part of her bowel is paralyzed."

This statement was not true. I would mull over these words later and wonder if he knew, even as he told me these things, that he had made a mistake that could kill her.

It took the doctors many phone calls and several hours to find a hospital that would accept her. Her condition was becoming worse by the hour. Finally, they got a hospitalist in Wichita to coordinate things; Air Evac Lifeteam transport was called, and soon she and I were flying to Wichita, two hundred miles away.

The Lifeteam was super. The paramedic, Laura, sat close beside Beth, supporting her on her knees, because the gurney was so narrow, Beth felt as if she might fall off. Beth had taken along Wink, one of her collection of small stuffed elephants, and Wink earned his wings on that flight, as Laura put the wings pin on his ear. Beth was awake and aware all the time. I was relieved when we landed in Wichita; she was transferred to an ambulance, and we got to St. Francis Via Christy Hospital—again.

It seemed to take forever for the evaluation and paperwork. Beth was so sick; she didn't feel like talking at all, so

I was answering their questions. (I know all of her medical history.) Soon another doctor came in, and he asked about doing a mental evaluation and an MRI of Beth's brain. He was asking why someone had ordered that when she was obviously so very sick. They said because she wouldn't talk to them!

She spoke up then and said, "I can talk. I just don't feel like talking."

The nurse said with a grin to the doctor who had been asking all the questions, "Maybe she just doesn't want to talk to *you!*"

The psychiatric doctor said he could see he wasn't needed, and he left. We didn't see him again.

When they finally got the paperwork done and a couple doctors had checked her over, they called us out into the hall and told us, "We don't think there is any way she can survive this, but we will do what we can."

Pointing upward, I replied, "And *He* will do the rest."

Thus continued what would prove to be a grueling, eight-week-long ordeal. Beth was sent downstairs for a liver scan, as they had been told she had a bile leak. Nothing was found. Later she was sent for another one, and I followed along. When I told the tech she had two JP drains, he was shocked, as nobody had told them that!

He said, "No wonder I can't find a bile leak!"

While we were there, my cell phone rang; it was Darrel telling me that Beth's sisters and their families were there. I said I thought we were about through and would be down in a minute. Beth said something I didn't catch, so I asked her what she'd said.

She replied, "You can't get any farther down; we're in the basement now."

I had no idea where we were! My mind was totally focused on Beth! I told her, "I'm going to keep you around; you'll keep me from getting lost!" It was amazing to me that even when she was deathly ill, her mind was perfectly clear.

SURROUNDED BY LOVE

—Beth—

I found out that my sister Kerri gives really good foot rubs! She gave me lymph edema massages that felt wonderful! She was very encouraging and also told me to stop trying to be so tough and to take pain medicine when I needed it. Both my sisters and their families stayed that first weekend, but they had to get home for their jobs.

Both Diane and Kerri came back the following weekend. It was wonderful to have the love and support of these two lovely young women. Kerri brought me a "care package" containing snacks, books, and other items she knew would be helpful to me. Diane brought a CD player and Christian CDs and a Bible. They were there during Beth's next big crisis, and I was so thankful to have them with me.

I had inquired about staying at the Ronald McDonald House, since the Perdue House where we had previously stayed was no longer in operation, and I was told there was a room available, and I could stay there as long as it was not needed for parents of a hospitalized child. I thank God for that place! They were wonderful to me, and when my daughters were there, they were allowed to stay there with me. There were two twin-sized beds in the room, and we could borrow another mattress for the third person. When Darrel was there, he stayed with me too.

The coordinating physician, or hospitalist, as they are now called, was a pleasant man named Dr. Dory Abou Jaoude. He always took time to talk to us, and after we felt we knew him a little, I asked, "Dr. Abou Jaoude, what is your nationality?"

He answered with a smile, "I am Lebanese, and my name means 'the father of goodness.'"

Isn't that a neat name for a doctor? He was a joy and a blessing, always willing to take time to answer our questions and make things easier in any way he could.

One evening I noticed a red patch about the size of the palm of my hand on the side of Beth's abdomen. The next morning, the redness had spread across her belly, and she also had red patches in the bends of both elbows and on both legs, above her knees, and was hot to the touch. I told the nurses about it, and they immediately informed the doctors, and tests were begun. She had two biopsies; one was red and bloody, the other was green. They said she had gangrene.

We were also told that Beth had necrotizing fasciitis. That is a horrible flesh-eating bacteria that can cause the loss of a limb in a short time or can cause death in many cases. I still do not understand for sure if it was necrotizing fasciitis or gangrene; different doctors told us different things, and still another said they are the same thing. But when I researched them, I found they are not the same. Since the main site of it was her abdomen, this was a very serious situation.

Beth was taken to surgery, where a huge incision was made and the dead and rotting flesh cleaned out. This incision was at least twelve inches long, and when they were finished cleaning her out, it was two-inches deep and went underneath the edges of the skin on both sides. This wound was left open.

Two days later, a huge abscess was found, and she was again taken to surgery for another cleanout. During this surgery, Dr. Jost discovered that there was a hole in her bowel. Dr. B. had perforated her bowel during the gallbladder surgery, and fecal matter had been invading and pumping through her system for *five weeks!* No wonder Beth was so sick! It is only because of the mercy of a loving God that she didn't die!

It appeared that in spite of everything being done for her, we were facing the loss of our precious daughter. I was so distressed and heartbroken, I couldn't even eat. I sat and hid my face behind Darrel's shoulder and cried while the rest of the family ate lunch in the hospital cafeteria.

When I found a chance to be alone and cry out to God, I pleaded with Him to spare Beth's life but added, "Father, I know you love my daughter even more than I ever possibly could, so if this is Your time to take her home to heaven, heal her body, allow her to dance on those streets of gold, use her hands any way she wants, then I am willing to release her."

After this prayer, I returned to her room and told Beth exactly what I had prayed, and then asked, "Now I need to hear from you—do you want to go home to heaven, or do you want to stay here?"

She answered without hesitation, "I want to stay here! I want to go to heaven, just not right now!"

"Well, all right, then! That's the way we will pray!" I answered.

Beth's answer and attitude reminded me of the confession in Psalm 118:17: "I shall not die but live, and declare the works of the Lord" (KJV).

During this time, I noticed that whenever I touched Beth, whether on her arm or face, anywhere, my hand smelled like a dead dog. It was appalling! I mentioned it to Kerri, and she said, "Well, Mom, it is dead flesh." I would have to wash and sanitize my hands every time I touched Beth.

The huge wound looked terrible. Beth was sent to the burn unit, and when I asked why, they said because they knew best there how to care for skin. She had a special nurse assigned to her around the clock, and two were available to bathe and change her. The nurses there were absolutely the best! Hardworking, caring, kind, compassionate—I cannot say enough to express our appreciation for the care they gave Beth.

During the second abdominal cleanout, a Malecot tube was placed in the hole in her bowel in order to drain the fecal matter. Each day, the wound was cleaned out, and it was packed with wet, sterile gauze. The nurses allowed me to stay in the room during these procedures. I had my camera handy at all times and documented in photos everything Beth was enduring. She never cried out or complained, even though the pain must have been awful.

We found it interesting and a bit amusing that the Malecot tube was flushed daily using 7UP! It took half a can, and when the nurse offered the remaining half to me to drink, I just couldn't drink it! But after a few more weeks, I did.

They became very concerned about Beth's nutritional needs. She had been able to eat next to nothing for almost five weeks following the gall bladder surgery; then for the next ten days, she had nothing but ice chips. She was literally on the verge of starvation. When they weighed her, we discovered she had lost over forty pounds! They put a tube down her nose and were feeding her through it, but they began strongly encouraging her to eat. They said "real food" was much better than the liquid nutrition she was being given.

The nurses asked her what she liked and what she wanted. She finally said she wanted some Bierocks (cabbage and hamburger baked in yeast dough rolls), so we asked if there was a place in the vicinity that made them. The nurse told us about a small place nearby that did, so we went and got her some. She was able to eat a little bit.

After she began eating a little bit and drinking Ensure, the nurses made her special treats, such as mixing Ensure with ice cream to make floats. They began replacing her depleted stores of potassium, calcium, and phosphorus, along with the various antibiotics. At one time, there were eleven bags of fluids hanging on her IV pole and going into her body. Darrel said it looked like a Christmas tree.

At her next liver scan, no more holes were detected in her intestines, and we praised the Lord. She was still so full of poisons that additional antibiotics were added. On

Sunday, June 7, she was pretty low, and she was started on oxygen, given one unit of blood, and had more chest X-rays. They now upgraded her status from extremely critical to "critical but stable."

Dr. Lancaster came in and told us he had two options: do a big midline surgery and try to repair the hole in her intestine, and do an ileostomy, which he didn't think she had strength enough to survive, or continue the conservative course of treatment she was on. We agreed to continue as they were.

Stool was coming out into the wound and also out the tube, and Beth had diarrhea. The doctor said she would be on antibiotics for a *long* time.

On the ninth day after Beth was taken from the care home to the hospital in Ulysses, the social services gal from the Legacy, as the care home had been renamed, called. She told me that their policy was that if a resident was out of the facility for ten days, all their belongings had to be removed, and they had to be dismissed.

Alternately, she would start having to pay $153 per day, private pay! We knew she would be there in Wichita for a long time yet, and she had no money to pay such fees. It would mount up to nearly $10,000 before she went home.

I was horrified and said, "It's not like she is on vacation! That is terrible! I need to be here with her, and you want us to move her out? Tomorrow?"

She was adamant, so I called Darrel, and he and Diane went and removed all Beth's things and took them to our garage. While they were doing that, I called and was talking to Diane. Jennifer Talbert, one of Beth's friends, who is a CNA at the home, came in and asked, "Why are you taking Beth's things? Did something happen?"

By now Jennifer was crying and wanted to talk to me, and she asked what was going on. When I explained, she said, "I don't think I even want to be here if Beth isn't here!"

It was a cruel and, in my opinion, unnecessary thing to do to our family, and it caused more heartache for all of us. And the thing we do not understand is that it has never been done to any other resident before or since that time, even though several have been out of the facility for longer than ten days. I must add that there is now a new administrator there and also a different social services person. I do not blame the social services person; she was only following orders.

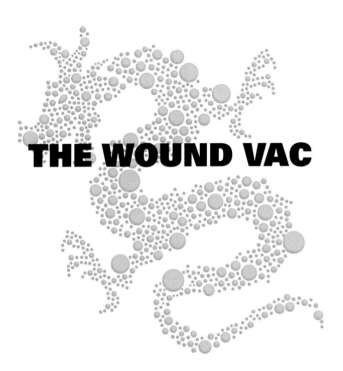

THE WOUND VAC

After the worst of the stool drainage stopped coming out through the big wound, they decided to put a wound vac on it. I had never heard of those before, but they are wonderful devices. First, a very open-pored, gray sponge, containing silver, is cut to fit into the wound. Then a dense, white sponge is laid over that, and the whole thing is covered with a sheet of what looked like very wide Scotch tape. A hole is cut in the tape, over the wound, and a flanged end tube is taped over the hole. This tube leads to a container. A vacuum pump is turned on, drawing the pus and impurities out of the wound, through the tube, and into the container. This greatly reduces the healing time.

There were two young male nurses working to install the wound vac on Beth, and both were sweating bullets, as they wanted to get it just perfect. An older female nurse was there supervising, I guess. She wasn't helping, just standing with folded arms, watching. There Beth was, totally naked, and this nurse's cell phone rang.

She listened a minute then said, "I'll be there as soon as we finish putting a wound vac on this guy."

Beth looked at me, and her eyes flashed! I knew what that was about, so I stepped over to the woman and said, "In case you can't tell, that isn't a *guy*. That is a woman!" Good grief. Then I picked up a clean, dry washcloth and laid it on Beth, saying, "Can't we at least give her a fig leaf?"

The two young men apologized and said, "Of course, we should have thought of that."

I kept a journal each day, beginning on June 9, 2009. Before that day, Beth had undergone so many surgeries and procedures. I will list some of them here: the initial gallbladder surgery; the installation of two JP drains; several liver scans; X-rays; surgery to fight gangrene; another to clean out abscess; nose tube for feeding; drains from wound; Malecot tube from hole in colon; pulling out and repacking gauze in wound daily; installing the wound vac; changing the wound vac sponges every other day. Then, of course, later came the pulling out of all the various tubes, but that was much easier.

When one is hospitalized and cannot move around much, a constant threat is having fluids build up in the lungs. Beth started breathing with a rattling sound, so breathing treatments were started. They did these every day, but she wasn't improving, so they also started percussion treatments. This involved "banging" her on the back with a mechanism on the bed to help jar the mucus loose.

After several days, she did improve and was able to discontinue the treatments.

Dr. Jost said he didn't intend to close the wound for at least ten days more after she began to improve. As it turned out, the wound never was closed, but it managed to heal on its own after several more weeks, leaving a scar about one-inch wide. The healing began at the bottom of the wound, filling in slowly with new flesh until it was just below the surface of the skin. It amazed the doctors; one told us he never thought that wound would heal. But God had plans for Beth, and He wasn't finished with her yet!

While Beth can no longer move anything except her head, her condition isn't true paralysis. In true paralysis there is no feeling in that part of the body. But Beth does have feeling all over her body; she feels pain when given shots, her feet are bumped, her arm is pressing too hard on the arm of her wheelchair, or any time something is done that normally would cause pain. She has suffered from headaches and leg and back pain for a number of years, requiring her to take a lot of strong pain medicines, which aren't always effective. Before being released from Via Christi, they tried to cut down the amount of meds she needed.

When Beth thanked her doctors for saving her life, they said they hadn't really done anything; her body just found ways to heal on its own. We know it was the healing power of God, and it brought to mind the words of a song titled "God Will Make a Way" by Don Moen:

> God will make a way, where there seems to
> be no way,
> He works in ways we cannot see, He will
> make a way for me.

Beth tried to eat as much as she could. But very often she would no more than finish a meal when it would come back up. Usually, I was the one near enough to catch it (keeping her from aspirating it) and dispose of it. Our wonderful chiropractor, Dr. Forrest Saxon, called and said to encourage her to eat cottage cheese, as it contains much-needed protein, so she did eat a few bites of that each day to please him, even though she dislikes cottage cheese. She could also eat cantaloupe, strawberries, small bites of chicken, and chocolate Ensure, all in small amounts.

Night sweats were another problem for Beth. She endured these night after night, and she was really glad when bath time came. (We think because of all the trauma her body had endured, these sweats signaled the onset of menopause.) She also enjoyed the first real shampoo she had had in weeks! They had been using the shampoo caps, but they just didn't feel the same!

GRATITUDE

I had purchased a small notebook, as I wanted to keep a "gratitude journal." I began to write down everything I noticed each day, for which we could be grateful. There were many, even in the midst of the storm. My entries include: great Lifeteam transport personnel; the Ronald McDonald House; kind, caring nurses; Beth being able to sleep; prayers of family and friends; my being able to come and stay with Beth; messages and cards from so many people; Diane and Kerri coming with their families; encouraging phone calls, and lots more.

The hospital has a website, and people could leave email messages for us on it. Each day, someone would bring us a little stack of those messages, and it was wonderful to know we were being thought of and prayed for during that time. It was gratifying to know she has so many friends who love her.

Thank God for cell phones! John called faithfully around 10:00 each morning, and I would hold the phone by Beth's ear so he could talk to her. He was positive and encouraging, and I believe his love had a lot to do with helping Beth keep on fighting. He kept telling her she had to get better, because he was coming for her birthday in August.

I was even thankful for all those long hospital corridors, as the only exercise I was getting was walking them plus walking back and forth from the Ronald McDonald House a couple times a day.

In some of those long corridors, those leading to the burn unit, were big, framed posters of Scriptures. I read those every time I walked those halls, which was many, many times. They encouraged me so much! The first one said: "Dear friend, I pray that you may enjoy good health and that all may go well with you" (3 John 1-2, KJV). Second one: "I will praise the Lord, who counsels me; even at night my heart instructs me" (Psalm 16:7). Third one: "He sent them to heal the sick" (Luke 9:2). Fourth: "May the eyes of your heart be enlightened that you may know the hope to which he has called you" (Eph. 1:18). The last one, and my favorite during those dark days, read, "Be not afraid…the Lord will be your confidence" (Proverbs 3:25-26).

On one of his trips to see us in Wichita, Darrel and I purchased a laptop computer so that I could stay in contact with my many friends online. What a blessing that was!

As soon as they learned I had it, they began to contact me often, and I shared all their messages with Beth.

I am inept with the computer but have wonderful grandsons who are great at it! Curtis was living in Los Lunas, New Mexico, at this time and was able to set up everything I needed on the new laptop remotely. I was really happy to be back in contact with family and friends.

Darrel had gone home, and even though I wanted so much to see him, I didn't ask him to come back to Wichita for my birthday in June. But that morning, I was talking to the nurses in the hall outside Beth's room, looked up, and there he was! With a glad cry, I threw myself into his arms, telling the nurses, "It's my *husband!*" Never had I been happier to see anyone!

He smiled and said, "I thought you might need to see me."

When we stepped into Beth's room, she grinned at Darrel and said, "You do things *right*, don't you?"

Diane had ordered a fruit bouquet for my birthday, and it was really something to see! Beth and I made quick work of those chocolate-covered strawberries. Darrel ate the honeydew slices, and we all three shared the rest. It was so sweet of Diane to remember me that way, and I have really nice pictures to remember her special gift.

MOVING OUT
OF THE BURN UNIT

R ight after the Fourth of July holiday, several more
burn patients were admitted, mostly due to acci-
dents involving fireworks, so they needed Beth's
room, and she was moved from there to Medical ICU.
They moved her during the hours I was at the Ronald
McDonald house, and when I walked into her former
room in the morning, she was not there! There was a man
in the bed!

I was shocked and scared, but the nurse rushed to assure
me that Beth was all right; she had only been moved. She
stayed in Medical ICU for several days, and then she was
moved to Select Specialty Hospital, a hospital-within-
a-hospital on the sixth floor. Select Specialty is an acute

long-term care hospital. This was considered "swing bed" so that Medicare would continue to pay her expenses.

Her same doctors continued caring for her, but of course she had a new staff of nurses there. There weren't as many nurses in that area, so I wound up doing a lot of her care and helping them when they were trying to turn her, bathe her, etc. Since I was spending a minimum of twelve hours a day there anyway, I didn't mind at all.

In Select Specialty, they brought in a bed for Beth that had a mechanism that turned her partially, first to one side and then the other, continually. This was to help her circulation and to prevent any pressure sores from forming. At first the bed didn't work properly. They worked on it several times and then finally noticed it was set for a patient who weighed 289 pounds! Since Beth weighed around 150, her weight wouldn't activate the mechanism.

While in the burn unit, Beth could not receive any flowers, but once she was moved, she got some lovely ones: red roses and white calla lilies from John, a lovely bouquet from our church, and a huge bouquet of balloons from her friend Becki, whom she met at the NF camp.

The hostesses at the Ronald McDonald House were all so kind to me, and I soon thought of them as friends. Each evening when I came back from the hospital, they inquired about how Beth was doing. One day when there had been more than the usual number of problems, one of them told me, "Just remember—if you don't have the *test*, you won't have the *testimony!*" How true those words are!

The first several days we were there, I used the service provided by the hospital of having the security drivers take me to and from the hospital, but I soon decided I needed the exercise and fresh air I got by walking instead. Several of the drivers showed me such compassion during the trying days when we didn't know if Beth would live or die. One lady looked at me in the rearview mirror as she arrived at the house and asked, "Do you need a hug?" And she jumped out of the car to give me one!

Another driver inquired about my patient and then pressed a little silver pocket "guardian angel" into my hand to keep as a reminder that we were not alone. Their kindness was such a balm to my hurting heart.

Beth was in several different rooms during this eight-week-long hospital stay. Her last room was on the fifth floor, and her window overlooked the rooftop where the helicopters landed, bringing more patients to the hospital. That provided some distraction as well as more people for whom to pray. We could also see the ambulances arriving on the ground below. Her doctors teased her about having to chase her all over the hospital! Via Christi is a very good, very busy hospital.

Beth was having lots of nausea and often threw up everything she ate. Her stomach was having trouble adjusting to having food in it, I guess. She also developed an itchy rash, and her infection doctor changed her meds, as she thought there might be an allergy to some of them. She had a whole team of doctors assigned to her, and each one was special and appreciated.

For several months after losing the use of her right hand, she could still drive her power chair with her left, and we had the control moved to the left side. The continuing decline in her mobility eventually had her driving erratically and she had to give up the last bit of personal freedom of movement she had. When she went for the gallbladder surgery, Beth still had use of her left hand. She could feed herself, change channels on her TV, get a drink of water from her nearby cup, etc. But this awful nightmare robbed her of even that little bit of mobility. Now she couldn't use her hands at all; she could not even turn over in bed. Her poor, twisted hands just lie crossed in her lap, and she has to ask for them to be switched so the other one is on top.

When she started getting grumpy and asking, "When can I go home?" we knew she was feeling better. Her doctors and nurses were willing to work with us to get her home as soon as possible. Around June 10, 2009, I was told she may get to go home in about another week, so I knew we must make arrangements to get her back into the care home in Ulysses or find another place for her. As it turned out, she didn't leave Select Specialty until almost a month later.

I called Darrel and asked him to come take me home so I could make the arrangements needed. He came on June 12. I was home for two days, during which time I went to the care home to see my mother, who had the room next door to Beth's former room. Beth's room had been given to a man after her things were removed. There was, at that time, only one empty room in the facility, which was on the 200 hall. Beth felt strongly that she didn't want to be on 200, as her favorite nurse and her favorite CNAs were on the 400 hall.

I talked to my mother about it and asked if she would be interested in looking at the empty room, and if she liked it, possibly moving into it and letting Beth have her room. She said she wanted Beth to come back there and for her to be happy, so she would move and let Beth take her room. This was a very unselfish thing for Beth's ninety-two-year-old grandma to do, and she really appreciated it. We talked to the director and made the arrangements.

Arrangements were also made for an ambulance to come to Wichita and transport Beth back to Ulysses as soon as she was released.

I happened to be at the Ulysses hospital while I was home, and Dr. B. stepped out and barred my way, asking, "She still up there?" Of course he meant Beth.

I said, "Yes, she's still there; I just came home for a couple of days to make arrangements for when she comes home."

He said he had been talking to several of Beth's doctors. "They are saying we made a hole in her colon. We didn't make it; they made it. Either that, or her colon just broke down on its own."

I was shocked, almost speechless! Then he looked at me and added, "And you're all she's had to depend on all these years." I do not understand what he meant, but I do understand that he did not want to own up to the responsibility that was his for puncturing Beth's colon and then not following up in any way to help her.

A friend from church was driving to Wichita to catch a flight and agreed to give me a ride back to Wichita. Once more, I was able to stay at the Ronald McDonald House, which had become my place of refuge. Each time every room filled up and it appeared I would have to move, a family left and I was able to stay. How I praise God for that place!

After nearly fifty days of hospitalization, they began to bring a Barton Chair into Beth's room each day. This is a special chair that reclines flat and adjusts to various degrees of sitting. She had been lying supine (on her back) for so long that they had to get her body accustomed to being in a more upright position. They had her sit in this chair for an hour each day. Beth said it was good to see things from a different angle and be able to see more than sky when she looked out the window.

It was almost another month before Beth was released. There were more minor complications and more conferences with the director of nursing at the Legacy in Ulysses concerning what had to be done before she could again be admitted there. We appreciate all the effort her doctors made to ensure Beth a smooth release and return to Ulysses.

Critical Care Transport sent one of their ambulances to pick us up. They had kindly said I could ride home with them, saving Darrel another four-hundred-mile round trip to pick me up. As they were loading Beth in the ambulance, I heard the attendant telling her that he had brought some "chick flicks" for her to watch on the way home. She said she watched *Fireproof* and another movie. They also stopped to buy Beth a Dr. Pepper to drink.

On the way home, the driver brought me up-to-date on all the happenings in our town during my absence. We appreciated the kindness of the ambulance team and just the normalcy of the conversations. Our arrival back at The Legacy seemed rather anti-climactic, as she had expected a big welcome, but everybody seemed to be too busy to notice her arrival.

In the following days, Sondra, Linda, and the other caregivers took very good care of Beth, making sure her wound was clean and dressed, and that the opening left from the Malecot tube was clean. The scar that formed was really big and angry looking, but with time, the redness has faded, and it isn't at all bad now.

Beth was readmitted to The Legacy in Ulysses on July 22, 2009. Her birthday is August 28, and John was coming, so we planned a birthday party for her in her neighborhood at The Legacy. Many friends and relatives were invited, and quite a few were able to come. And friends from other neighborhoods (halls) of the care home that Beth knew were also invited.

She received many cards, flowers, and gifts. Her cakes were ice cream cakes, her favorite, and on one it said, "Happy Birthday, Beth," and on the other, "We're Glad You're Still Here!" It was truly a celebration of the healing power of God and the life of a special person. John sat beside Beth, and her friend Becki, who had driven all the way from North Dakota to be there, sat on the other side and opened her gifts for her. Beth couldn't stop smiling that day!

For the past several years, when John comes to visit Beth, we just hand him the keys to the special van we purchased so he can take her places. Since they can't be away from The Legacy too long, they go out to eat (John has learned to alternate taking a bite of his food, then giving Beth a bite of hers) to movies, to the museum, whatever he can think of to entertain themselves. This works very well.

LIFE GOES ON

One of the things we are most thankful for is that all who are entrusted with her care at The Legacy are kind and loving. They all care about Beth and go out of their way to do things for her. Her disability is so complete that she cannot scratch any itch, change the channel on her TV, answer or hold her phone, or feed herself. She can literally do nothing. So it is vital that they are instantly available when she calls. Her call light is a gadget that is clipped to her clothes, under her chin, and she can just bump it with her chin when she needs something.

Her poor hands are twisted into unnatural positions and she can only lift the left one a few inches with intense effort. Her feet are turned in at sharp angles and try to cross, making it difficult to get her comfortable in a wheelchair. The chair she is using is not comfortable for her; it is long, heavy, and hard to maneuver, but we continue taking her places because she is worth the effort.

She enjoys having Darrel and me pick her up and take her to Sunday school and church each Sunday. And being out among other people is really good for her. Many of our church family go out of their way to greet her; some have known her for years.

The CNAs who care for her are good about offering her water each time they come into her room, asking her what she wants to watch on TV, answering and clipping her phone to her shoulder when she has a call so she can talk, all simple things but so very important.

The girls also bring her special treats to eat (the entire staff there knows her tastes!). Even the administrator finds things she knows Beth likes and brings them to her. They spoil her, and Beth and I both love it!

After she had healed up from all the surgeries and trauma of the last hospital stay, we noticed several changes. Her hair, which had become like straw, dull, dry, and lackluster, gradually regained its natural curl and shine. Her complexion cleared up, and her color improved. And, the greatest of all these blessings, she became pain-free for one of the first times in her life!

She asked me, "Mom, when am I going to get my miracle?"

My answer was that she *had* gotten a miracle! Not having headaches is so wonderful! And since the meds for those causes constipation, with the attendant problems that brings, it is a double blessing to be pain-free! After she thought about it, she agreed that it was a miracle. She remained mostly pain-free for about a year. Some of the headaches have returned, along with leg pain, but not as much as before.

Recently, as I walked toward Beth's room, I was stopped by the social services lady, who asked, "Does Beth have Jawbreakers [candy] in her room?"

I said I thought she did, and she told me Beth had asked for one the night before, was given one, and then left alone. She accidentally sucked it into her airway and nearly choked on it. She wasn't able to activate her call light, but she finally coughed the Jawbreaker up. Scary!

She said Beth would probably take it better for me to take those away than for them to do it. So, of course, I took all her Jawbreakers and Atomic Fireballs out of the room! This is an example of the extent of her disability and also the protection of the One Who loves her most.

Beth is still childlike (but not childish) in a lot of ways. She loves candy and has a drawer full of it, but she doesn't really eat it that much. I guess she just likes having it there. She is easily pleased by small things: a flower, a small stuffed toy, a balloon, a card, a phone call. She never nags at me if I get busy and miss a day or two of visiting her (I try to go every day, but sometimes life interferes). She always expresses her pleasure at seeing me walk into her room, and she is appreciative of everything anyone does for her.

Recently, Beth told me she needed to talk to me about something. Her serious expression got my attention, and I asked, "What?" She said she wanted to apologize for the way she acted and the way she blamed me for her having to go to the nursing home.

I told her I understood completely and had never held that against her in any way. This is typical of Beth; she likes to keep short accounts and not have bad feelings about anything she or anyone else has done.

Beth first asked me if I could write a book about her life about four years ago. I didn't really realize she was serious about it, but she asked me again each year until I finally said, "You know, Beth, I believe I can do that!" We talked about titles, and she chose *Beauty for Ashes* (which we eventually weren't able to use for publication reasons). When I asked her reason for liking it, her answer was, "For years, it seemed my whole life had turned to ashes; but now it is a thing of beauty." What an inspirational statement, from someone so totally disabled. Only God can receive the glory for Beth's astounding attitude!

The people who take care of Beth and cook for her are all so special. She loves and appreciates each one, and she looks for opportunities to compliment them on the work they are doing. Everyone likes to be appreciated, and these girls like spending time in Beth's room, just hanging out with her, visiting, talking, teasing, joking, and just enjoying her. They often spend their breaks with her, because that is more enjoyable than going to their break room.

John finds really different kinds of things to send her. For one birthday, he sent her a heart-shaped, engraved acrylic tribute reading:

> Dear Sweet Beth,
>
> I thank God every day for bringing you into my life. Before I met you I thought love would never find me. I think about you every day. You are truly the sweetest and most wonderful person to ever come into my life, everything about you is wonderful. I love your smile, I love your laugh, I love watching you eat. You have a great sense

of humor. You are a warm, loving lady. You have a strong, great faith in the Lord. I could fill a library with all of your good qualities, and couldn't write one line about your bad ones. I love you so much, and I am happy that you feel the same way about me. Thank you for being mine.
HAPPY BIRTHDAY
8/28/10

Love, John

John knows Beth loves pigs and recently he sent her a T-shirt with a big, pink pig looking shocked and saying, "Harry? Is that you?" while looking at a sweating, crying, strip of bacon. She loves that shirt and wears it every time it returns from the laundry.

Another engraved acrylic tribute arrived for Valentine's Day in 2011. This one reads down the left-hand side: "Because of You" and then:

B

E

T

The day you stepped into my life was the day you stole my heart. Meeting you was the greatest single event in my life. As bad as having neurofibromatosis is, and can be, it has been worth it, because without it, I'd have never had the joy of knowing you. If I said Thank You every minute of every day for a thousand years, I could not thank you enough for being mine. I can't wait to see you and your beautiful smile again. Remember always that I love you deeply.

H

With my deepest love, John
2/14/11

LOOKING TO THE FUTURE

As we look to the future, Beth continues to amaze all who know her. Her attitude is continually one of optimism; she is sweet and kind to all with whom she comes in contact. She listens to a lot of Christian teaching via TV and audio discs, and she constantly strives to improve her outlook. Recently, she told me that she wants to stay on an even keel, to not be up one day and down the next.

Whenever a nurse or CNA tells Beth she is having a problem (just in visiting) or she knows they are in pain, Beth offers to pray for them. This touches their hearts, and they love her for it.

"Faith is the victory," says an old gospel song, and how true are those words! Faith in the God of all healing, love, and mercy has brought us through everything the enemy has thrown in Beth's path. Her name means "my God is abundance," also "consecrated to God," and this expresses her life so well.

While visiting her a short time ago, we were talking about things for which we are grateful. The very first thing Beth mentioned was "breath." And she is truly thankful for every breath God allows her. Other things she mentioned were: life; family and friends who love her (she has many!); home; a bed; a sound mind; an ability to talk, see, hear, and laugh; her caregivers; freedom; and, something I hadn't considered, her arms and legs, even though they don't work anymore (her words).

As we worked on this book, I asked, "Beth, when you were so terribly ill that last time in Wichita, were you ever scared?"

Her answer was, "No."

That surprised me a little, so I asked why, and she answered, "I couldn't die; I'd just gotten to love and be loved by John, and he said if I died before him, he would be crushed."

While we understand that, as things stand now, it would not be possible for John to take care of Beth, she is still holding to the healing promises in the Word and believing she will be able to stand and walk down the aisle to become John's bride. They talk about "when we get married" and continue to love and respect each other in spite of all the obstacles. But we cling to the promise from Luke 1:37 (KJV): "For with God, nothing shall be impossible!"

I have never seen a love like theirs, one in which there has never even been a kiss on the lips, only hugs from him and kisses on the forehead, but you can see the love shining in their eyes. They inspire me. John comes to Kansas to visit her as often as he can. She counts the days before each visit, having the girls chart the days remaining on a dry-erase board in her room. And he calls her every day.

As she faces the future, Beth's unquenchable spirit and faith shine as a beacon, inspiring many others to trust in Him who has delivered her from the pit, not once, but time and time again.

"Thank God in everything, no matter what the circumstances may be, be thankful and give thanks; for this is the will of God for you who are in Christ Jesus" (1 Thessalonians 5:18, AMP).

"The Lord is my light and my salvation—whom shall I fear? The Lord is the stronghold of my life—of whom shall I be afraid? For in the day of trouble, He will keep me safe in His dwelling; he will hide me in the shelter of His tabernacle and set me high upon a rock" (Psalm 27:1-2, 5, NIV).

Adversity introduces man to himself.

—Unknown

AFTERWORD

More children are affected with NF than are affected by cystic fibrosis, muscular dystrophy, and Huntington's disease combined. One in every 2,500 children born is affected with NF. However, it does not receive a proportional share of money for research, a problem we pray will be corrected. Some celebrities have given time and effort to fundraising for NF, and their efforts are sincerely appreciated, but much more is needed. Where there are organized chapters of NF, they do fundraisers like car races and other things. Many NF families also do special fundraising events in their own areas.

A portion of the proceeds from this book will be given to neurofibromatosis research.

If you want more information on any of the forms of NF or would like to contribute funds for NF research, you may contact the following:

Neurofibromatosis, Inc. (NF Inc)
P.O. Box 66884
Chicago, IL 60666
nfinfo@nfinc.org
http://www.nfinc.org
Tel: 630-627-1115
800-942-6825

Children's Tumor Foundation
95 Pine Street
16th Floor
New York, NY 10005
info@ctf.org
http://www.ctf.org
Tel: 800-323-7938 or 212-344-6633
Fax: 212-747-0004

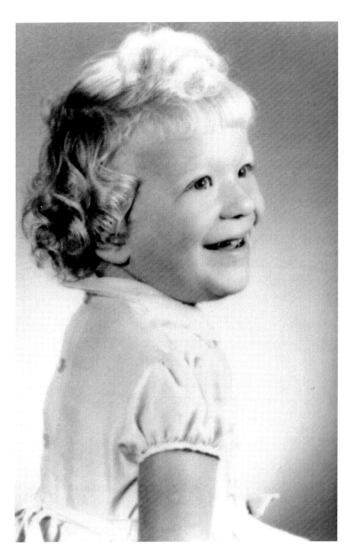

Beth at two years of age, 1964

Beth's fifth grade photo, 1972

Janet and Beth, 1979. Beth is ready for the Junior Prom

"Nanny" Beth with Liz and Matt, Virginia, 1990

Senior Portrait 1980

Janet and Darrel, 1982

Beth's wrecked car, 1997

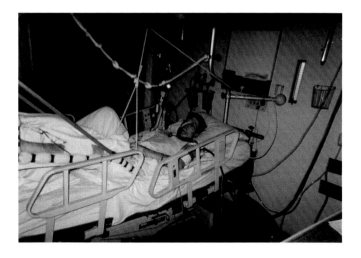

In traction in hospital after 1997 car wreck

Beth's "family," December 2000

Diving with her own dive guide, Cozumel 1991

Scuba diving in Honduras 1999

Piloting the Honky Tonk in Honduras 2001

John and Beth at Nebraska Land Rodeo, June 2004

John and Beth at Boot Hill, Dodge City, June 2004

Dear Darrel,
When you married mom
I really didn't know what to
think of you now you didn't
know what to think of me either
I was just thankful you
were sent to be with mom.
We've had a lot of ups and
downs since then
I'm proud to have you as
a dad you've gone beyond duty
as a step-dad. Since my
disability has gone from bad to
worse you've not thrown
in the towel but have stayed
encouraging to both mom and I.
You out did yourself in Jan
when I spilled the boiling water
on myself. You came over helped
me get socks and pants & put
ice on burn. You called 911
and got mom notified. Then you
stayed until I left. Thank you
for all you've done & do.
I love you, Beth

Letter to Darrel, 2005

Dear mom

Thank you for being
My mom. Knowing I was
a little diff from siblings
after age 4 but you Never treated
me different or made a big
deal about it.

In 1997 when I was in
car wreck you put your life
on hold so you could help get
me through a close tragedy
all those days I was in
ICU you hung on to Gods
outstretched hand and to his word.
You Sang to me, Cried with me
& held me in your arms.
you Never let me give into the
pain and told me "Show satan
that what he intended for bad God
will use for good. Now my
disability has reared its ugly head
and you've been more than Encouraging
& supportive. In fact when I burned
my self I could see the concern on your
face. Thank you for all you've done

Letter to Janet, 2005

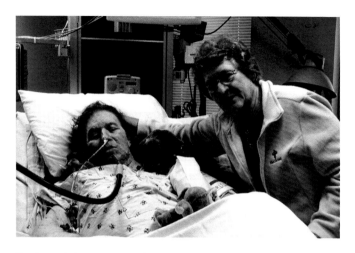

Beth and Janet at Via Christi Hospital, Wichita, May 2009

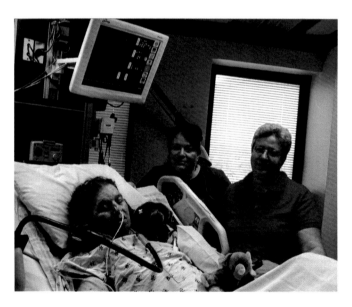

With sisters Kerri and Diane, Wichita, May 2009

Special friends: Mindi, John, and Becki with Beth, August 2009

Photo for National Nursing Home Week, May 2011

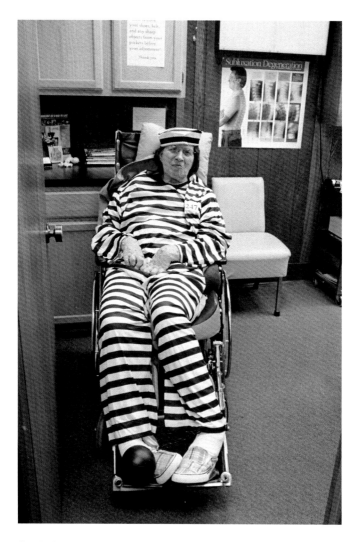

Beth in her Halloween costume from John, October
2011 (Convict costume, complete with ball and chain!)